AMISH QUILTS
THE ADVENTURE CONTINUES

FEATURING 21 PROJECTS FROM TRADITIONAL TO MODERN

Edited by Lynn Koolish

C&T PUBLISHING

Text, Photography, and Artwork copyright © 2013 by C&T Publishing, Inc.

Publisher: Amy Marson

Creative Director: Gailen Runge

Art Director: Kristy Zacharias

Editors: Lynn Koolish and Jill Mordick

Technical Editors: Doreen Hazel and Teresa Stroin

Cover Designers: Kristen Yenche and Kristy Zacharias

Book Designer: Kristen Yenche

Production Coordinators: Jessica Jenkins and Rue Flaherty

Production Editor: Joanna Burgarino

Illustrator: Tim Manibusan

Photo Assistant: Mary Peyton Peppo

Photography by Diane Pedersen of C&T Publishing, Inc., unless otherwise noted

Published by C&T Publishing, Inc., P.O. Box 1456, Lafayette, CA 94549

Library of Congress Cataloging-in-Publication Data

Amish quilts : the adventure continues : featuring 21 projects from traditional to modern / Edited by Lynn Koolish.

pages cm

ISBN 978-1-60705-791-8 (soft cover)

1. Patchwork--Patterns. 2. Amish quilts. I. Koolish, Lynn.

TT835.A484 2013

746.46--dc23

2013009775

Printed in China

10 9 8 7 6 5 4 3 2 1

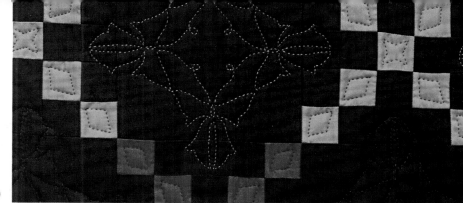

contents

preface

As we approached our 30th anniversary at C&T, it was an easy decision to do a book on Amish quilts to celebrate. It was also a no-brainer (as they say) to include the two women who were involved with C&T Publishing from the beginning: Carolie Hensley (the "C" of C&T) and Roberta Horton, author of C&T's first book, *An Amish Adventure*. Fortunately, both of them were happy to be involved.

Our goal for this book is to present a collection of quilts that celebrates and honors Amish traditions and the influence of Amish quilts over the years. We did a call for submissions and selected quilts that we felt represented a broad spectrum, from Amish-made traditional quilts to modern interpretations that reference Amish quilts in new and unexpected ways.

In the process of selecting the quilts, we were thrilled to see how many contributors had either taken a class from Roberta Horton or worked through the exercises in her book on their own.

We're so glad you'll be along as we continue the adventure.

foreword

By Carolie Hensley

"Thank you for the opportunity to review your business proposal. Unfortunately we are unable to approve your loan. We wish you the best of luck in your endeavors."

Those were the words we heard from more than one bank when we set out to establish C&T Publishing and publish our first book. It was early in 1983, and Roberta Horton, a popular local quilt instructor, was teaching a class on Amish quilts at the Cotton Patch, my quilt shop in Lafayette, California. One day, Roberta mentioned that she wanted to write a book on Amish quilts but did not yet have a publisher. I quickly replied, "Roberta, we will do that."

I thought, how hard could it be to publish a book? That evening, I presented the idea to my husband, Tom—Roberta has a manuscript for a book on Amish quilts, and she wants us to publish it for her. When Tom responded that he didn't know how to be a publisher, I sent him off to the library. He found a book on self-publishing, which he read several times from cover to cover, each time becoming more intrigued by the possibilities. Next, he enrolled in a course on publishing at the University of California at Berkeley and determined that it would take an initial investment of $25,000 to publish Roberta's book.

The next challenge was figuring out where to find $25,000. The first stop was the local bank. It seems that they didn't like the idea of having 10,000 copies of a book as collateral for a loan. Rather than being dejected, we became more determined than ever to prove the banks wrong. We set out to find ten friends willing to invest $2,500 each to launch the book. We raised the $25,000 within two weeks, created a limited partnership, and began our new publishing company. Of course, the fledgling company needed a name, and in case you hadn't guessed, we chose C&T for Carolie and Tom.

Now that we had the money, we had to make Roberta's book a reality. In the fall of 1983, we (Carolie, Tom, and Roberta) went to Quilt Market in Houston with little more than a printed book cover and a photocopy of the book pasted inside. We took enough orders to cover the expenses and headed home to finish the book.

Before long, 10,000 copies of the book were delivered from the printer directly to "company headquarters"—our garage, living room, and even bedrooms were converted to a warehouse with boxes of books, shipping materials, labels, tape, and blank invoices. At that point, our life really changed. Tom came home from work and spent his evenings packing orders, while I typed invoices and took books to the post office for shipment the next day. *An Amish Adventure* was selling very well, and C&T Publishing was shipping books all over the United States. We paid back the original investing partners and dissolved the partnership.

To keep the momentum going and to make C&T's order form look more impressive, we started publishing more books. Eventually the house filled floor to ceiling with boxes upon boxes of books.

Our sons, Tony and Todd, both recall returning from college to find their bedrooms overtaken with boxes. Navigating from room to room resembled running a maze. Todd joined the company full-time in 1988 and, with Tony, helped move the operations out of the house and into an office and warehouse facility. The house was back to normal. At the time, the warehouse seemed enormous, but within a few years, C&T was again bursting at the seams and soon moved to a larger building. In 1989, Tony joined the company full-time, and Diane Pedersen was hired as C&T's first full-time employee. Tom and I decided it was time to let go of the reins and agreed to sell C&T to Tony and Todd.

Over the past 30 years, C&T has built an extensive list of best-selling titles as the company continues to set the industry standard for beautiful, high-quality books and products. This would never have been possible without the untiring effort of all the C&T employees, freelancers, and authors.

Thank you to Roberta Horton, the initial investors, and everyone who is a part of the C&T success story. It has been one amazing journey—happy 30th anniversary to everyone at C&T!

~Carolie Hensley

P.S. In case you were wondering, the first employee, Diane Pedersen, still works at C&T.

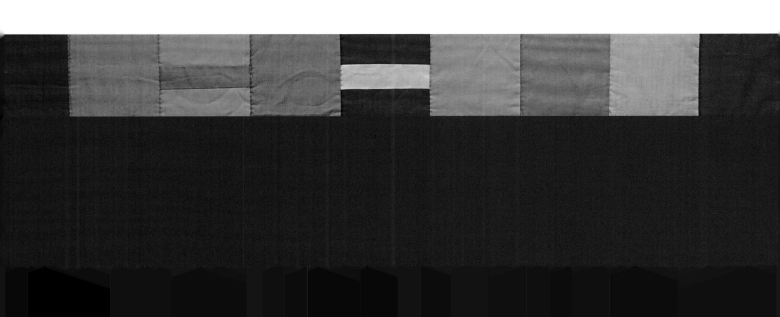

introduction:
what makes a quilt amish

By Roberta Horton

What makes a quilt Amish? Technically, it must be made by a person who is a member of the Amish religion. Historically, these quilters used only solid fabrics. The quilts look plain and stark when compared with similar ones made by the "English," the term used by the Amish to describe their non-Amish neighbors. The quilts are pieced from geometric shapes; there is no appliqué, and construction is simple. For example, mitered corners are not used in the borders; instead, the borders, as well as the bindings, have butted corners. An Amish quiltmaker works within the restrictions set by her or his church district.

But many of us non-Amish quiltmakers like to make Amish-style quilts because we love the way they look and the intense feelings they evoke. We, therefore, are making Amish-inspired quilts in which we closely follow their rules or restrictions.

The most important guideline is that in traditional Amish quilts, only solid fabrics are used, as prints are considered too worldly. In a few *rare* instances, an Amish quilter may include a few pieces of printed fabric, but that doesn't give us permission to do so if we are making an Amish-inspired quilt. (*Note:* Many present-day Amish do make quilts with printed fabric to sell to the "English.")

The Amish tend to work with simple patterns. Lancaster County (Pennsylvania) Amish are known for their starkly simple Diamond-in-a-Square, its variations, and Bars, in which they use large pieces of fabric. Their Sunshine and Shadow quilts look like a plain version of Trip Around the World. Other communities use rectangles to make Bricks, Streak of Lightning, Chinese Coins, and Log Cabins. Repeat patchwork blocks—one pattern and block size per quilt—are common in the Midwest. Again, simple.

Amish quilts have wide borders, which are good places for quilting designs. The simple quilts of Lancaster County are known for their lavish quilting in the large plain areas. Their quilts often feature feathers in the wide borders, which can have corner blocks—fancy quilting with simple construction. Midwestern quilts usually have more pattern pieces per quilt and feature narrower borders without corner blocks, so there is less room for fancy quilting. Cables, fans, and diagonal lines replace feathers—simple quilting with fancy piecing. Both cases are a good example of using contrast.

Color selection is determined by community or region. What is important is that the Amish employ dark, medium, and light values in their quilts. The overall effect is that Amish quilts, in general, are darker than most non-Amish quilts. However, there are wonderful surprises within the quilts themselves, that I call *sparkle*, *glow*, and *fade out*, which are found in some, but not all, Amish quilts.

Sparkle

This visual effect occurs when pale, clear, light colors are placed next to, or are surrounded by, dark colors. A lightish-value fabric becomes lighter yet when surrounded by a darker fabric. The light fabric appears to bleach out because of the contrast between the two. The effect is maximized when the greatest difference in value within the quilt is between the fabrics used. Sparkle is used as an accent, so it should appear in less than 50 percent of the blocks; otherwise, it won't stand out as something special. Examples in this book include *Amish Star* (page 12), *Ocean Waves* (page 31), *Repeat Block on Point* (page 17), *Sparkle* (page 22), and *Amish Memories* (page 20).

Glow

Glow occurs when a clear medium fabric is placed next to or surrounded by a dark value. This can happen within a block or when an inner border is a medium, clear bright and the outer border is dark so the lighter area looks illuminated, or glowing. Technically speaking, glow is sparkle grown up one value. If you have a medium fabric and put light around it or with it, the medium value becomes darker. If instead you surround the clear medium fabric with dark, the medium becomes lighter. The medium fabric becomes the opposite of what you surround it with. Examples include *Ocean Waves* (page 31), *Repeat Block on Point* (page 17) and *Amish Chinese Coins* (page 28).

Fade Out

Fade out happens when two fabrics of similar value are placed next to each other. They end up reading as one larger fabric. Fade out, which is a characteristic of Amish quilts and scrap quilts, can add interest and variety to a quilt and is an excellent example of how contrast in value is necessary for defining shapes and patterns. Examples include *Triangle Treasures* (page 21), *Amish Star* (page 12), *Repeat Block on Point* (page 17), and *Thankful* (page 18).

The quilts in this book run the gamut from traditional Amish-made quilts to Amish gone modern.

Amish Quilts—Quilts made by members of an Amish community

In the Style of Amish Quilts—Quilts made following Amish traditions by people who are not members of an Amish community

Inspired by Amish Quilts—Quilts inspired by Amish quilts; you can clearly see the influences, but these quilts break with the traditions

Capturing the Essence of Amish Quilts—Quilts that may or may not look like Amish quilts, but their simplicity captures the essence of Amish quilts

Beyond Amish—Quilts that are inspired by some element of Amish quilts, such as color schemes, but that otherwise don't look like Amish quilts

Amish Gone Modern—Quilts that use simple Amish patterns, but not Amish colorations, such as a white background. A perfect formula for a modern quilt—everything old is new again …

gallery

amish quilts

Quilts made by members of an Amish community

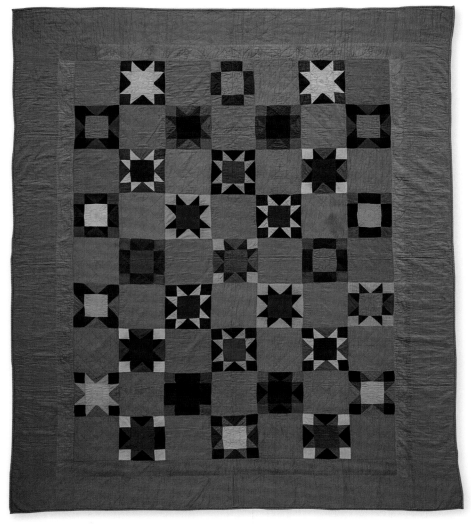

Amish Star, Kalona, Iowa, antique traditional Amish, 78″ × 92″, from the collection of Roberta Horton; Pieced and hand quilted

This quilt was collected in Kalona, Iowa, where there's a large Amish community. *Amish Star* is a good example of a scrap quilt made from many fabrics. Although only one patchwork pattern is used for all the blocks, many variations can be seen because of the way the background values of the corner squares and the perimeter triangles of the individual blocks are used. Some variations are more pleasing than others. Roberta feels that the purpose of the ugly, or more awkward-looking blocks is to make the more attractive blocks appear better yet in comparison.

Some blocks also contain very light fabrics, which adds a sparkle effect (page 10) to the quilt and makes the blocks special, emphasizing the implicit understanding that effects such as this should be used as an accent. If all the blocks were special, then none would show as special.

All in all, this quilt exemplifies the Amish traditions that Roberta loves.

Bow Tie, Ohio Amish c. 1930, 70″ × 84″,
from the collection of the San Jose Museum of Quilts & Textiles

This quilt is an example of Ohio Amish quiltmaking at its zenith. The manipulation of color is particularly representative; and the quilt includes cotton sateen fabrics, as do many Ohio Amish quilts from this period.

Ocean Waves, 46″ × 46″, 1998, from the collection of Peggy Martin; Machine pieced and hand quilted; Purchased in 2000 from a dealer of Amish quilts. The quilt was made in Lancaster County, Pennsylvania. In the quilting are the initials "MG" and the date 1998.

Color is the first thing Peggy notices when looking at a quilt, and the colors in Amish quilts have always inspired her. She is drawn to the clear, bright solid fabrics that are used in Amish quilts, and she particularly loves the way different bright colors vibrate when placed against each other, as well as how all those bright colors glow against the darker ones. These color interactions have made her look at fabric in new ways and have greatly influenced her style.

This quilt radiates the qualities of sparkle and glow (page 10).

in the style of amish quilts

Quilts made following Amish traditions by people who are not members of an Amish community

Sawtooth Diamond-in-a-Square by Annette Anderson, 46" x 46", 1985; Pieced, hand quilted

Annette was first inspired by Amish quilts because of their graphic impact and bold colors. The stark simplicity of design has always been aesthetically appealing to her. She feels that Amish women have taken their limitations of pattern to an extreme art form by their use of color and that their manipulation of limited colors, bold or muted, shows their individuality and genius.

This inspiration influences Annette as she selects fabrics for quilts, putting one fabric next to another and observing how each color impacts the other in its value and intensity. This realization has continued to have a great influence on her quiltmaking to this day, as her favorite part of making a quilt is choosing the fabrics for each project.

Garden Railway Amish Bars by Anabeth Dollins, 3⅝″ × 3½″, 2000; Machine pieced (paper piecing) and hand quilted

Whether scaled up to bed-size or down to mini-mini-size, Amish quilts always look elegant and eye-catching. Anabeth is inspired by the contrast of black and jewel tones and the simple geometry of Amish designs. These mini-mini quilts, which show that inspiration, are based on traditional Amish designs—Center Diamond-in-a-Square and Amish Bars—but are sized to fit into a quilt show diorama in a garden railway.

Garden Railway Lancaster County Center Diamond by Anabeth Dollins, 3½″ × 3½″, 2000; Machine pieced (paper piecing) and hand quilted

Taking several classes on Amish quilts from Roberta Horton, working through her book *An Amish Adventure*, and viewing the Esprit collection of Amish quilts were turning points in the development of Reynola's quilting style. From these experiences came the sense of possibility and the freedom to use many different fabrics—qualities that have influenced nearly all the quilts she has made over the past 30 years. Reynola has been able to create designs by controlling the selection of fabric values, the positioning of values, and the selection of colors and color clarity. The use of low-contrast designs, as in this quilt, has become the focus of her work.

Each block in this quilt uses a different fabric for the design, with the background fabric held constant, yet there is much to look at. The sparkle (page 10) grabs your attention, while the fade out (page 10) draws you in for a closer look.

Repeat Block on Point by Reynola Pakusich, 42˝ × 52˝, 1987; Machine pieced and hand quilted

Thankful by Candyce C. Grisham, 44″ × 60″, 1991,
from the collection of Pat Forget; Pieced and hand quilted

Candyce has always been inspired by the simplicity, symmetry, and beauty of
Amish quilts—the use of solids is so traditional and yet so contemporary. She
has also admired the hand quilting and the quilting designs. She learned to
quilt using cardboard templates, hand piecing, and hand quilting. Although she
now does machine piecing and quilting and uses rotary cutters, she continues
to find ways to include the traditional in her contemporary designs.

This traditional Ocean Waves pattern—half-square triangles arranged in light,
medium, and dark patterns—makes good use of fade out (page 10).

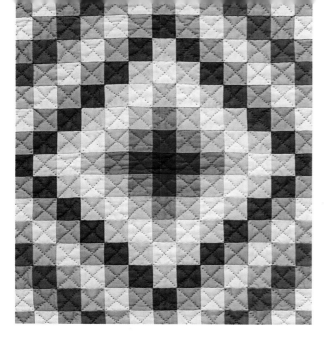

Valerie made this Sunshine and Shadow quilt after she took Roberta's Amish class in the 1980s. It features a dark-medium-light color gradation using 27 solid colors. This quilt is an excellent example of sparkle (page 10).

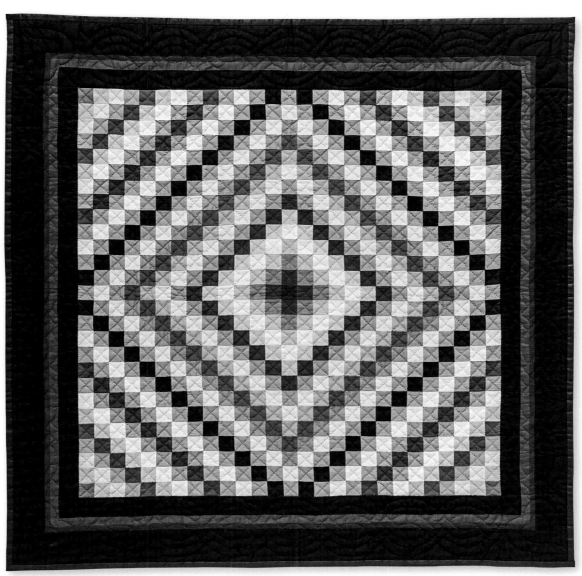

Sunshine and Shadow, pieced by Valerie Yeaton, quilted by an Amish quilter, 54″ × 54″, c. 1980

Amish Memories by Susan Vachino, 73″ × 85½″, 2012; Pieced and machine quilted

After viewing the Esprit collection of Amish quilts, Susan realized how powerful simple things, such as uncomplicated shapes and solid fabrics, can be. Even with a limited color palette, the Amish quilters were able to create surprising and rich color combinations. Stepping closer to the quilts revealed another delight as Susan took in the beautiful quilting designs. She knew she had to make a Double Nine-Patch quilt based on her favorite quilt in the collection.

Susan didn't find any published patterns that included the inner border of squares on point, so she designed her own, using tips from Roberta Horton's *An Amish Adventure* to help with color placement. In the process, she created a color scheme that has all three qualities of sparkle, glow, and fade out (page 10). Susan adapted Froncie Quinn's quilting stencils (based on another Esprit quilt) for the machine quilting.

This Double Nine-Patch is Susan's tribute to Amish quilters and what they taught her about the craft.

inspired by amish quilts

Quilts inspired by Amish quilts; you can clearly see the influences, but these quilts break with the traditions

Triangle Treasure by Ilene Bartos, 67″ × 88″, 2012; Machine pieced and quilted

Ilene has always loved Amish quilts, especially the stunning beauty of their simplicity and richness of colors.

This pieced Ocean Waves quilt, with its gradation of color and fancy border (which make it Amish Inspired rather than In the Style of Amish), is a wonderful example of the Amish influence on today's quilters. Especially effective is the way the darker areas of the quilt make use of fade out (page 10).

In 1985, Bonnie discovered Roberta Horton's *An Amish Adventure*. She joined a group that was studying Amish quilts using Roberta's exercises, and they spent the next year exploring and working with solid colors. During that time, Bonnie learned much more about value, the aesthetics of happenstance, sparkle, and fade out (page 10). As her quilts have developed since then, she has leaned more and more toward using solid, or solidlike, fabrics. Bonnie has been dyeing her own fabrics since 1977; her study of Amish design and color use gave her subsequent dyeing work a direction and sensibility that it would not have had otherwise.

This quilt used Roberta's lesson on making Nine-Patch blocks with sparkle.

Sparkle by Bonnie M. Bucknam, 46″ × 46″, 1985; Machine pieced and hand quilted

capturing the essence of amish quilts

Quilts that may or may not look like Amish quilts, but their simplicity captures the essence of Amish quilts

Machine pieced and quilted, this Four-Patch quilt is the essence of bare bones simplicity with a sparkle effect (page 10).

Nightfall by Bill Kerr and Weeks Ringle, 38″ × 38″, 2005
Photo by Bill Kerr

Elizabeth is drawn to Amish quilts because they seem to still the noisy world around her with their clear colors, high contrasts, and simplicity of design. Sometimes she thinks about what vision these Amish quilters had in their pure and simple way, and while she might want to romanticize their life, she recognizes that hard work produced this clarity of form. It's that message that sends her back to her own quilting, time and time again.

This Diamond-in-a-Square quilt clearly captures that essence of simplicity, especially the simple quilting that is perfect for this small quilt.

Square-in-a-Square Doll Quilt
by Elizabeth S. Eastmond, 15½″ × 15½″, 1986;
Pieced and hand quilted

beyond amish

Quilts that are inspired by some element of Amish quilts, such as color schemes, but that otherwise don't look like Amish quilts

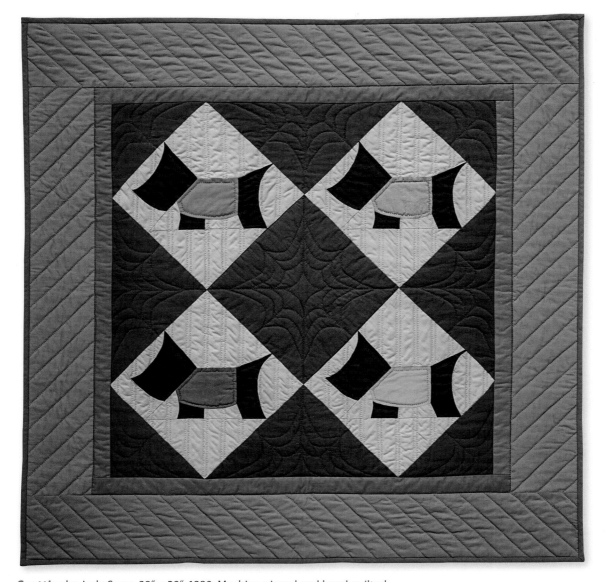

Scotties by Judy Sogn, 38″ × 39″, 1980; Machine pieced and hand quilted

This quilt is in a category of its own. Judy likes the simplicity of Amish quilts and particularly likes the color palette of the Pennsylvania Amish. She chose to use a nontraditional pattern in a traditional Amish manner, following guidelines from Roberta Horton's classes.

amish gone modern

Quilts that use simple Amish patterns, but not Amish colorations, such as a white background

Reflection of the Times by Angela Yosten, 40″ x 44″, 2013; Quilted by Natalia Bonner

This quilt was inspired by the orange reflective safety triangles that are on the backs of Amish carriages. The use of neutral solid fabrics makes the one orange triangle stand out from all the rest.

An Amish Picnic Quilt by Angela Yosten, 60˝ x 60˝, 2013; Quilted by Natalia Bonner

This quilt was inspired by the simplicity of Amish quilts and their use of solid fabrics. The red and white fabrics mixed with a traditional quilt design bring thoughts of outside picnics in the sunny weather.

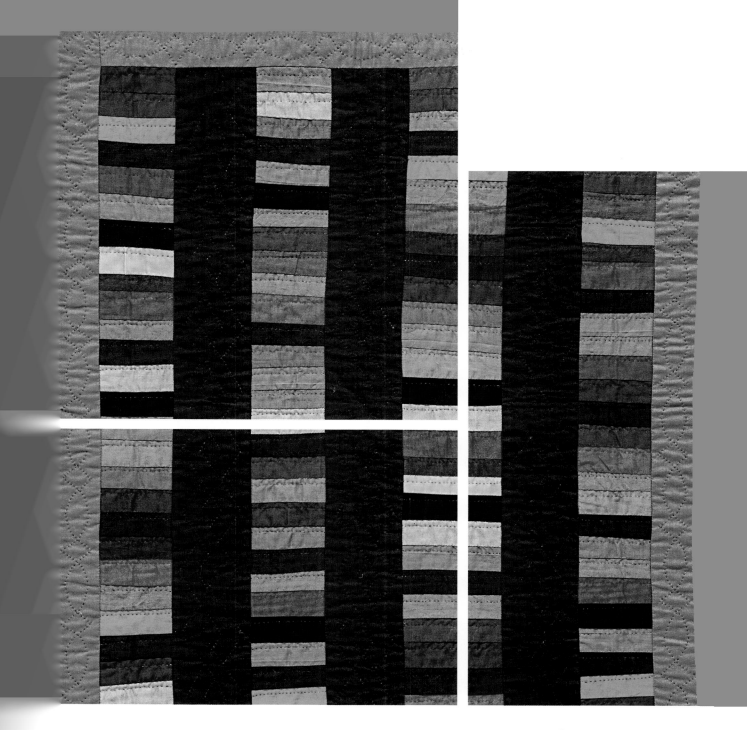

projects

amish chinese coins

FINISHED QUILT: 34″ × 38″

Antique Amish, Holmes County, Ohio, from the collection of Roberta Horton

MATERIALS

Wide variety of solids in small amounts for units (coins)

Blue solid fabric: ¼ yard for inner borders

Black solid fabric: 1⅛ yards for vertical sashes and outer borders

Binding fabric: ⅜ yard

Backing* and sleeve fabric: 1¼ yards

Batting: 40″ × 44″

*44″-wide fabric is required for the backing.

CUTTING

Wide variety of solid scraps

All coins must be cut 3½″ wide, but they should have varying heights of 1″, 1⅛″, 1¼″, 1⅜″, and 1½″.

Blue solid fabric

Cut 2 strips 2″ × 21½″ for horizontal inner borders.

Cut 2 strips 2″ × 28½″ for vertical inner borders.

Black solid fabric

Cut 3 strips 3½″ × 25½″ for vertical sashes.

Cut 2 strips 5½″ × 24½″ for horizontal outer borders.

Cut 2 strips 5½″ × 38½″ for vertical outer borders.

Binding fabric

Cut 4 strips 2½″ × 40″ for double-fold binding.

This Amish Chinese Coins quilt, collected in Ohio, exemplifies what Amish quilts are all about. It has wide borders; it is dark; and it uses solid-color fabrics. Corners are butted, not mitered. Construction is simple, with rectangular units (or "coins") set in vertical strips.

What is exciting is the way the color arrangement dances on the quilt's surface. Certain colors stand out, and our eye follows their seemingly random placement in the quilt. These colors *glow* because they are medium-value clear brights surrounded by darker values or duller colors. Some of the coins of equal value to the sashing strips seem to *fade out*, or disappear, into the background, acting only to fill a space in the strip. So color and value placement is one key.

Another big contributor to the excitement found in this quilt is that the coins weren't cut using a modern-day rotary cutter and a quilter's ruler. If they had been, all the coins would be the same size. Today's technique is to cut a designated-width strip across the fabric width or length. Next the strip is crosscut into a specified size of equal units. In this quilt, however, the coins were cut individually, probably from scraps. Only the width of the units is uniform. Technology allows us to be perfectionists but sometimes removes the excitement caused by randomness.

All in all, this is a wonderfully traditional Amish quilt, with great color use and simple construction. What more could a contemporary quiltmaker ask for in a quilt?

construction

Vertical Strip Assembly

1. Arrange the coins into 4 vertical strips in a random order on your design wall or a large flat surface. There will be 27–30 coins per strip, depending on the height of your coins. It may be helpful to place the 3 black sashes between the rows you are composing (they will appear to be too short). See which colors show the most. In the example quilt, these would be the red, green, and beige coins. Make sure that these colors don't line up horizontally across the quilt.

2. Sew the coins into 4 strips. The strips should be 25½″ long. Press all the seams in one direction.

Quilt Assembly

1. Arrange the 4 coin strips in their designed order on the design wall or on a flat surface. Add the 3 black vertical sashes.

2. Sew the 4 vertical coin strips to the 3 black sashing strips. Press the seam allowance toward the sashing.

3. Sew the 2 blue 21½″ inner border strips to the top and bottom of the quilt. Press the seam allowance toward the inner border.

4. Sew the 2 blue 28½″ inner border strips to the sides of the quilt. Press the seam allowance toward the inner border.

5. Sew the 2 black 24½″ outer border strips to the top and bottom of the quilt. Press the seam allowance toward the inner border.

6. Sew the 2 black 38½″ outer border strips to the sides of the quilt. Press the seam allowance toward the inner border.

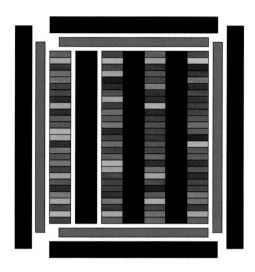

Quilt assembly

Quilting and Finishing

1. Mark quilting designs on the quilt top or plan to stitch without marking.

2. Layer and baste the quilt (see Layering and Basting in Quiltmaking Basics, page 123). Quilt by hand or machine.

NOTE

Some quilting suggestions: Use a cable design in the vertical strips, clamshells in the outer border, and add a line of quilting at the seams of the coins.

3. Bind the quilt (see Binding in Quiltmaking Basics, page 123).

4. Make and attach a sleeve, if desired.

about the collector

Roberta Horton has been a quiltmaker since 1970. She has taught and lectured internationally. In 2000, Roberta was the recipient of the Silver Star Award, presented by the International Quilt Association in Houston, in recognition of her lifetime body of work and the historic effect it has had on quilting.

Roberta's study and love of quilts has been the motivation for the development of her many workshops. Each workshop has provided her a means to explore a different type of fabric or to use color in a new way. She is the author of six quiltmaking books, including *An Amish Adventure: A Workbook for Color in Quilts*, which was C&T Publishing's first book.

Within the quilting world at large, studying the Amish use of color has proved to be a vehicle for gaining a deeper understanding of color interaction and how to use it. The Amish way of choosing the easiest construction methods and patterns has also flavored Roberta's personal style of quiltmaking.

ocean waves

FINISHED BLOCK: 8″ × 8″ | **FINISHED QUILT (as shown):** 44″ × 44″

Made by Suzanne Keeney Lucy

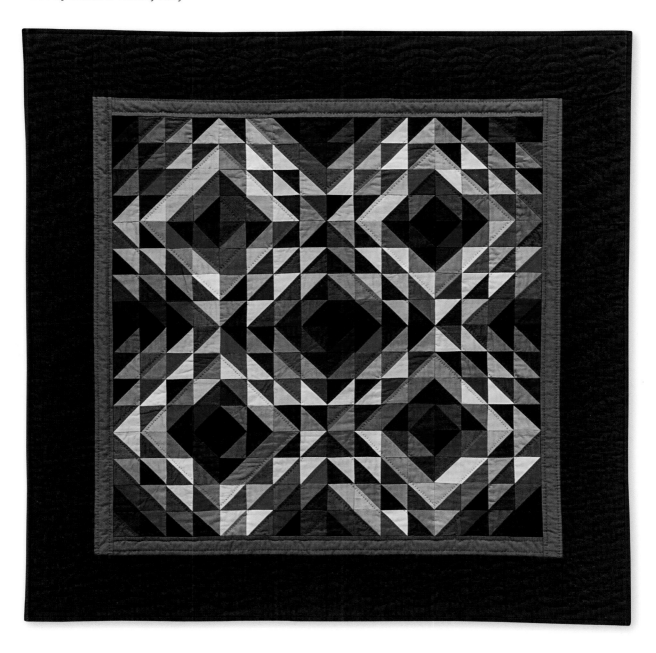

Fortunately for me, my study of Amish quilts began early in my life as a quilter. I say fortunately, because I learned to value the beauty and impact of simple patterns and saturated colors. Initially, the colors in Amish quilts, the purples and blues, the cooler side of the color wheel, appealed to me. They were the colors of my clothing and my favorite colors, so I was comfortable with using them. Being a beginning quilter, I also appreciated that the simple patterns were easy to piece. But I soon realized there were other reasons Amish quilts were so intriguing.

As I collected books on the Amish and studied their quilts, the subtle complexity of their designs and color placement and combinations made them even more interesting to me. So much is "hidden" in those simple designs. It might be the several different blacks in the background or a renegade red triangle in a sea of blues or a pattern of contrast that glows when the lights are turned low. Whatever it was, I found that I never got tired of looking at them.

I have explored many styles and techniques and have taken classes from talented teachers, but I often return to the Amish quilts with renewed interest and appreciation. In 1997, I had the opportunity to see the Esprit collection of Amish quilts at the San Jose Museum of Quilts and Textiles in California. What an experience to see these quilts in person! I was once again moved to create an Amish-inspired quilt, this time using the "warm" colors of the Midwestern Amish palette.

I have tried in my own work to achieve simplicity of style in combination with creative visual interest. I hope that one sees in my quilts the honesty and artistry that I have found in Amish quilts.

MATERIALS

Solid-color fabrics: A variety in a range of values from very dark through medium-dark, medium, and medium-light for half-square triangles; Use scraps and pieces from 3″ × 3″ up to 3″ × width of fabric to total 2 yards.

Blue solid fabric: ⅜ yard for inner border

Dark purple solid fabric: ⅞ yard for outer border

Binding fabric: ½ yard black solid

Backing fabric: 3⅛ yards

Batting: 51″ × 51″

CUTTING

Solid-color fabrics

Cut 256 squares 2⅞" × 2⅞".
Cut each diagonally once to
make 512 half-square triangles.

Blue solid fabric

Cut 4 strips 2" × width of fabric
for inner border.

Dark purple solid fabric

Cut 5 strips 5" × width of fabric
for outer border.

Binding fabric

Cut 5 strips 2½" × width of fabric
for binding.

construction

Block Assembly

1. Arrange 32 triangles into a
block, paying careful attention to
value placement. Place the darkest
triangles in opposite corners (top
left and bottom right as shown
in the block assembly diagram,
below). Place the medium-dark,
medium, and medium-light
triangles in the center. Refer to the
quilt photograph (page 31) to help
with your placement choices.

2. Sew pairs of triangles
together along the long edges.
Press. Sew half-square triangles
together to form a block. Press.
Make 16 blocks.

Block assembly

Quilt Assembly

1. Arrange and sew blocks in 4 rows of 4 blocks each, rotating every
other block so that the diagonal seams alternate direction from block to
block. Press. Sew the rows together. Press.

2. Cut the inner border strips into 2 pieces 2" × 32½" and 2 pieces
2" × 35½".

3. Cut 2 of the 5 outer border strips into 2 pieces 5" × 35½". Sew the
remaining 3 strips together end to end. Cut this strip into 2 pieces
5" × 44½".

4. Sew on the top and bottom inner borders first and then the side
inner borders. Repeat this sequence for the outer borders (refer to Butted
Borders in Quiltmaking Basics, page 123).

Quilt assembly

Quilting and Finishing

1. Mark quilting designs on the quilt top or plan to stitch without
marking.

2. Layer and baste the quilt (see Layering and Basting in Quiltmaking
Basics, page 123). Quilt by hand or machine.

3. Bind the quilt (see Binding in Quiltmaking Basics, page 123).

4. Make and attach a sleeve, if desired.

about the quiltmaker

Suzanne Keeney Lucy has been playing with fabric and art since she was a young girl. Her grandmother bought her a Singer Featherweight sewing machine when she was ten years old. As she and her grandmother sat side by side, Suzanne learned to sew. She remembers an early interest in fabrics, looking through bolts in the basement of the local department store. She earned a degree in psychology, even though she avoided studying in college by experimenting with papier-mâché, macramé, needlepoint, batik, and photography.

Suzanne grew up in upstate New York but kept moving west until she settled in the Pacific Northwest. For the past 40 years, she and her husband have lived and raised their three children in a river valley in the foothills of Mount Baker.

After dabbling in pottery, she turned to her love of fabrics and sewing and found her passion—quilting. She appreciates the stories behind the tradition of quilting, and she loves working with her hands to create either functional bed quilts or art pieces. Recently, she has been experimenting with surface design techniques to create her own fabrics. Her work is inspired by nature, supported by her family, and influenced by other artists.

bear paw

FINISHED BLOCK: 8¾″ × 8¾″ | **FINISHED QUILT:** 49⅛″ × 49⅛″

Made by Judy Sogn

I chose a block pattern and a color scheme that I felt would represent choices an Amish woman might make. I included several reds and pinks, from pale pink to dark maroon, including a grayed maroon to reflect the Amish tradition of using leftover fabrics from clothing construction. The background fabrics also include a variety of blacks, and the dark maroon is used as a background in one of the blocks.

MATERIALS

Pink/red solid fabrics: A variety to total ¾ yard for Bear Paw blocks

Black/dark solid fabrics: A variety to total 2 yards for Bear Paw blocks

Black solid fabric: 1⅜ yards* for setting squares and triangles, corner squares, and borders

Pink solid fabric: ¼ yard* for inner border

Maroon solid fabric: ½ yard for binding

Backing fabric: 3⅓ yards

Batting: 55″ × 55″

* Requires 42″ usable fabric width

CUTTING

For each Bear Paw block

Note: For each of the 9 Bear Paw blocks, choose 1 pink/red fabric and 1 black/dark fabric.

Pink/red fabric:

Cut 1 square (A) 1¾″ × 1¾″.

Cut 8 squares (B) 2⅛″ × 2⅛″ for half-square triangles.

Cut 4 squares (C) 3″ × 3″.

Black/dark fabric:

Cut 4 squares (A) 1¾″ × 1¾″.

Cut 8 squares (B) 2⅛″ × 2⅛″ for half-square triangles.

Cut 4 rectangles (D) 1¾″ × 4¼″.

For quilt assembly

Black solid fabric:

Cut 5 strips 4½″ × width of fabric for outer borders.

Cut 4 squares 9¼″ × 9¼″ for setting squares.

Cut 2 squares 13⅝″ × 13⅝″. Cut each diagonally twice for 8 side setting triangles (E).

Cut 2 squares 7⅛″ × 7⅛″. Cut diagonally once for 4 corner triangles (F).

Pink fabric:

Cut 4 strips 2½″ × width of fabric for inner border.

Maroon fabric:

Cut 6 strips 2½″ × width of fabric for double-fold binding.

construction

Block Assembly

1. Layer 1 pink (B) square and 1 black (B) square with right sides together.

2. Draw a diagonal line from corner to corner on the top square.

3. Sew a ¼″ seam on each side of the drawn line.

4. Cut on the drawn line to make 2 half-square triangles. Press seams toward the black fabric.

5. Repeat Steps 1–4 to make 16 half-square triangles.

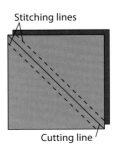

Half-square triangles

6. Arrange the pieces for each block and stitch together.

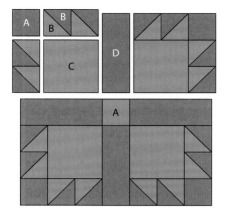

Bear Paw block

7. Repeat Steps 1–6 to make 9 Bear Paw blocks.

Quilt Assembly

1. Arrange the blocks, setting squares, and setting and corner triangles on your design wall or a large flat surface.

2. Sew the blocks, setting squares, and setting and corner triangles together in diagonal rows. Press the seams in alternate directions from row to row.

Sew diagonal rows together.

3. Sew the diagonal rows together. Press seams toward the bottom of the quilt.

4. Measure, cut, and sew the pink inner borders to the quilt—side borders first, followed by top and bottom borders (refer to Butted Borders in Quiltmaking Basics, page 123).

5. Measure, piece as necessary, cut, and sew the black outer borders to the quilt, as in Step 4.

Quilting and Finishing

1. Mark quilting designs on the quilt top or plan to stitch without marking.

2. Layer and baste the quilt (see Layering and Basting in Quiltmaking Basics, page 123). Quilt by hand or machine.

3. Bind the quilt (see Binding in Quiltmaking Basics, page 123).

4. Make and attach a sleeve, if desired.

roman stripe for alison

FINISHED BLOCK: 8½″ × 8½″ | **FINISHED QUILT:** 65″ × 82″

Made by Janet Duer Smith

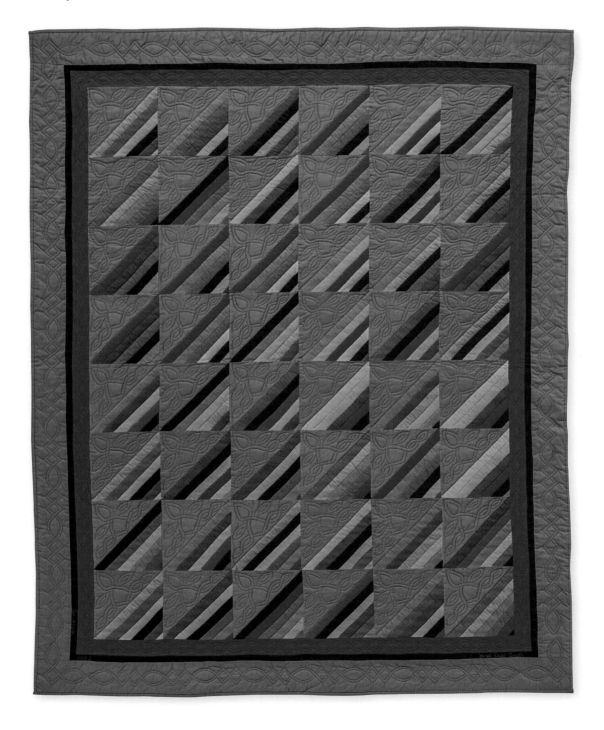

I made this quilt in 1982. After all of these years, I am still drawn to the graphic design and clear, bold colors of this Amish-inspired quilt. I am most touched by the thought of the Amish women working together to design such lively and spirited quilts, with their forceful quilt designs juxtaposed with their simple, routine lives. In the early 1980s, we used many of the same techniques that were used by these Amish women. Rotary cutters were not available, so I marked my fabric using a ruler and cut the strips with scissors. We also hand quilted our quilts on a frame; the designs I used were taken from traditional Amish quilts. The templates I used for this quilt were hand cut by Jane Toro. Just like the Amish quilters, my quilt group, including Barbara Gaffield, Bess Chin, and Jane Toro, came to my house at night to stitch. And, after all of these years, we continue to spend time quilting together.

MATERIALS

Solid-color fabrics: 9–12 assorted ¼- to ⅓-yard pieces to total approximately 3 yards for stripes

Teal solid fabric: 3½ yards for half-square triangles, outer border, and binding

Rust solid fabric: ⅝ yard for inner border

Black solid fabric: ⅜ yard for middle border

Backing: 5¼ yards

Batting: 71″ × 88″

CUTTING

Solid-color fabrics

Cut strips 1½″ × width of fabric to total 60 strips for stripes.

Teal solid fabric

Cut 6 strips 9⅜″ × width of fabric; subcut each strip into 4 squares 9⅜″ × 9⅜″. Then cut each square diagonally once for 48 triangles.

Cut 8 strips 4½″ × width of fabric for outer border.

Cut 8 strips 2½″ × width of fabric for binding.

Rust solid fabric

Cut 7 strips 2½″ × width of fabric for inner border.

Black solid fabric

Cut 7 strips 1½″ × width of fabric for middle border.

construction

Block Assembly

1. Sew together 6 solid-color 1½″ × width of fabric strips. Avoid using 2 strips of the same color in any given set. Press seams in one direction. Make 10 strip sets.

Strip set—Make 10.

2. To begin cutting striped triangles from the strip sets, align a 45° line on your quilter's ruler along the left edge of a strip set. Trim.

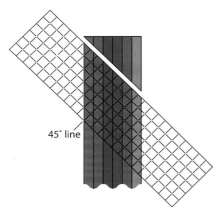

45° line

Ruler placement

3. Rotate the ruler or flip it upside down. Again align a 45° line along the left edge of the strip set. Place the ruler's right edge 13¼″ from the trimmed left edge of the strip set. Cut along the right edge. *The resulting triangle will not have a point at the top, but the slight missing area will not affect construction.*

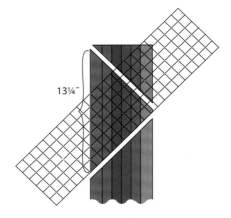

13¼″

Rotated ruler placement

4. Rotate the strip set and repeat Step 3 for a total of 5 striped triangles per strip set. You will have 2 extra striped triangles.

Make 5 triangles per strip set.

5. Sew the long edge of a striped triangle to the long edge of a teal triangle. Press the center diagonal seam in the same direction as the striped triangle seams. Repeat to make 48 blocks.

Completed block—Make 48.

Quilt Assembly

1. Arrange and sew together the quilt rows.

NOTE

Measure your quilt (as described in Butted Borders, page 125) before cutting your borders to size. For each border, sew the sides first and then the top and bottom.

2. Sew the rust color strips for the inner border end-to-end. Cut into 2 strips 2½˝ × 68½˝ and 2 strips 2½˝ × 55½˝.

3. Sew the black strips for the middle border end-to-end. Cut into 2 strips 1½˝ × 72½˝ and 2 strips 1½˝ × 57½˝.

4. Sew the teal strips for the outer border end-to-end. Cut into 2 strips 4½˝ × 74½˝ and 2 strips 4½˝ × 65½˝.

5. Sew on the inner border, the middle border, and the outer border (refer to Butted Borders in Quiltmaking Basics, page 123). Press toward the borders.

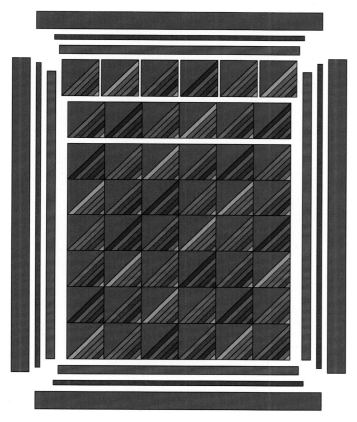

Quilt assembly

Quilting and Finishing

1. Mark quilting designs on the quilt top or plan to stitch without marking.

2. Layer and baste the quilt (see Layering and Basting in Quiltmaking Basics, page 123). Quilt by hand or machine.

3. Bind the quilt (see Binding in Quiltmaking Basics, page 123).

4. Make and attach a sleeve, if desired.

about the quiltmaker

Janet Duer Smith has been quilting since 1976, when she first took a quilting class at Albany (California) Adult School from Roberta Horton. Janet is a charter member of East Bay Heritage Quilters, a group that was formed from Roberta's classes in the San Francisco Bay Area. Although Janet has favored traditional, geometric quilts in the past, she has recently produced more modern, pieced collage quilts. The part of quilt-making that gives her great joy is working with color. Recently she has taken up machine quilting baby quilts that she makes for family and friends, but she still enjoys taping up her index finger, donning her thimble, and putting that hand-sewing needle into the fabric.

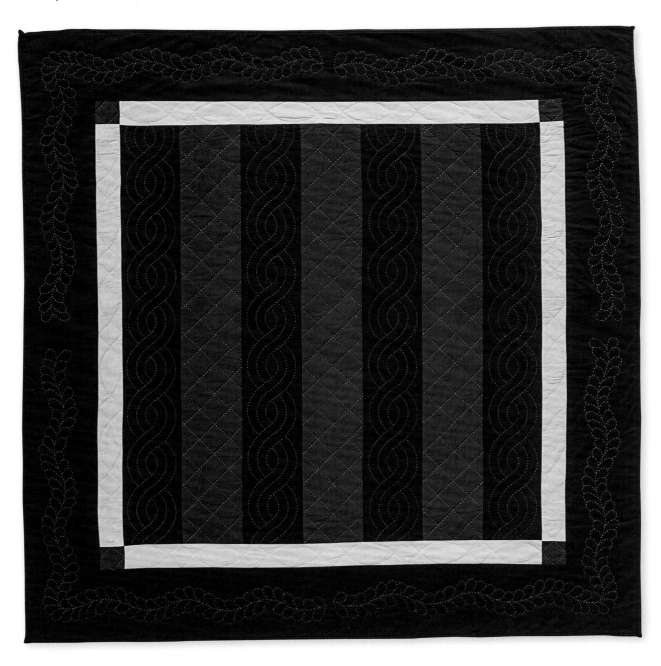

electric amish

FINISHED QUILT: 51″ × 51″

Made by Julie Brown Neu

It all started with the thread. When I discovered thread that glows in the dark, I bought a few spools immediately and then tossed them into my thread drawer to wait until the right project came to mind. I knew that the quilt would need to have a plain design and plain fabrics to allow the quilting to shine. With its simple designs, solid fabrics, bold colors, and exquisite quilting, an Amish-style quilt was the obvious choice.

I have always been drawn to Amish quilts. As a Quaker, I share a theologically based aesthetic with the Amish community, preferring items that are plain, but beautifully made. I appreciate that many Amish quilts achieve great beauty without relying on vibrant fabric patterns or intricately pieced designs. Through simple strips, squares, and jewel-toned fabrics in purples, teals, reds, and blacks, Amish quilters can create quilts that practically glow. Still, as a hand quilter, I also cannot fail to admire the striking designs wrought in thread in the background.

With *Electric Amish*, I used Amish quilts as my inspiration, but I also diverged from tradition with an ironic twist. I chose a simple, traditional bars design and typical solid black and purple fabrics. I used common quilting designs, though I mixed designs generally found in Lancaster with those often used in the Midwest. I also quilted *Electric Amish* entirely by hand. My deviation comes with my thread choice. Not only have I used a light thread against the dark black and purple fabrics, but I used thread that glows in the dark when exposed to electric light. Without electricity, this feature of the quilt would be lost in an Amish home.

MATERIALS

Black solid fabric: 4⅞ yards for bars, outer borders, backing, and binding

Dark purple solid fabric: ¾ yard for bars and inner border corner squares

Light purple solid fabric: ⅜ yard for inner borders

Batting: 57″ × 57″

Quilting thread: Glow-in-the-dark thread

CUTTING

Black fabric

Cut 1 piece lengthwise 40″ × 57″ for backing center.

Cut 2 strips lengthwise 10″ × 57″ for backing sides.

Cut 2 strips lengthwise 6½″ × 51½″ for side outer borders.

Cut 2 strips crosswise 6½″ × 39½″ for top and bottom outer borders.

Cut 4 strips crosswise 5½″ × 35½″ for bars.

Cut 6 strips crosswise 2½″ × width of fabric for double-fold binding.

Dark purple fabric

Cut 3 strips 5½″ × 35½″ for bars.

Cut 4 squares 2½″ × 2½″ for inner border cornerstones.

Light purple fabric

Cut 4 strips 2½″ × 35½″ for inner borders.

construction

Quilt Assembly

1. Sew the long sides of the black and dark purple bars together, alternating colors. Press toward the purple bars.

2. Sew 2 of the 2½″ × 35½″ light purple strips to the top and bottom of the bars strip set. Press toward the black bars.

3. Sew a dark purple square 2½″ × 2½″ onto each end of the 2 remaining light purple strips. Press toward the dark purple squares.

4. Sew the light purple inner borders with the corner squares to the sides of the bars strip set.

5. Sew the 2 black 6½″ × 39½″ outer border strips to the top and bottom of the center section.

6. Sew the 2 black 6½″ × 51½″ outer border strips to the sides.

Quilt assembly

Quilting and Finishing

1. Mark quilting designs on the quilt top or plan to stitch without marking.

2. Sew the 2 backing strips 10″ × 57″ to the backing center 40″ × 57″ to complete the backing.

3. Layer and baste the quilt (see Layering and Basting in Quiltmaking Basics, page 123). Quilt by hand or machine.

4. Bind the quilt (see Binding in Quiltmaking Basics, page 123).

5. Make and attach a sleeve, if desired.

TIP

This quilt uses white glow-in-the-dark thread for the black bars and outer borders and pastel purple glow-in-the-dark thread for the purple bars and inner borders.

about the quiltmaker

Though she dabbled in sewing as a child, Julie Brown Neu did not become a quilter until after she finished college. A few days before graduation, she decided she would need a hobby to fill the hours of free time that would replace studying. She bought a couple of books, pulled out a pair of scissors and a needle, and started quilting. In the many years since graduation, not only has she discovered rotary cutters, but also her quilting has gone from being a hobby to an absolute passion.

Julie began her quilting pursuits with traditional, hand-quilted bed quilts. She has since expanded her repertoire to include art quilts and their various techniques, such as fusing, painting, and dyeing. She currently teaches and lectures about quilting and sells her work through www.julieneu.com. Julie, her husband, and their infant daughter split their time between Boston and western Massachusetts.

anna's four-patch doll quilt

FINISHED BLOCK: 3″ × 3″ | **FINISHED QUILT:** 22¼″ × 26½″

Made by Laura Mattox

I love Amish quilts. I'm inspired by their bold, rich colors set against an austere black background. I enjoyed pulling out my collection of solid fabrics in various colors to make my doll quilt. There was no pressure in finding the perfect print or scale in the fabric. And there was no dashing out to the nearest quilt shop to find that one particular print. It seemed like child's play—simply pick out many colors and let them do the work! There really was no wrong fabric choice, because the black background took care of any color that I chose. I used what I had in my small box of solids and imagined that the Amish quilter of days gone by did the same. She used what she had in her scrap bag, perhaps cutting pieces from fabric used to make the family's clothing.

The hand-quilting stitches that show up so well in Amish quilts speak to me of the hours spent creating these beautiful works of art. I am also inspired by a relatively simple patchwork pattern coming to life with the elaborate hand-quilted cables, feathers, and other motifs that freely travel and fill in the spaces. Hand quilting an Amish quilt gives the quilter ample room to express his or her creativity through this timeless art.

Amish quilts appeal to me because they allow me to do what I love the most. I love to piece simple patchwork, and I love to hand quilt. The advantage of making an Amish quilt is that the precious time spent in hand quilting is often rewarded by those stitches really showing up. Amish quilts are simply mesmerizing, allowing the viewer to visit for a long while. There's a lot to look at in order to truly appreciate all the beauty an Amish quilt has to offer.

MATERIALS

Solid-color fabrics: 20–25 assorted pinks, blues, cheddar, greens, browns, reds, and purples, no smaller than 4″ × 4″ square for Four-Patch blocks

Black solid fabric: ¾ yard for setting squares, setting triangles, corner triangles, and outer border

Blue-gray solid fabric: ¼ yard for inner border

Red solid fabric: ⅓ yard for binding

Backing fabric: 1 yard

Batting: 28″ × 32″

Hand quilting thread: Gray and black

CUTTING

Assorted solid-color squares

Cut 4 squares 2″ × 2″ from each 4″ × 4″ square for a total of 80 squares.

Black solid fabric

Cut 12 squares 3½″ × 3½″ for setting squares.

Cut 4 squares 5½″ × 5½″. Cut each square diagonally twice for setting triangles. (You will have 2 extra triangles.)

Cut 2 squares 3″ × 3″. Cut both squares diagonally once for corner triangles.

Cut 4 strips 2½″ × width of fabric for black outer border.

Blue-gray solid fabric

Cut 4 strips 1⅛″ × width of fabric for inner border.

Red solid fabric

Cut 3 strips 2½″ × width of fabric for double-fold binding.

construction

Block Assembly

1. Choose 2 matching 2″ × 2″ squares. Select another set of 2 squares in a different color.

2. Sew the squares together into pairs as shown. Press the seam allowance toward the darker fabric. Sew the pairs together to make a Four-Patch block. Press. The block will measure 3½″ × 3½″. Repeat to make 20.

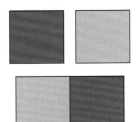

Make 20.

Quilt Assembly

1. Arrange the 20 Four-Patch blocks to make 5 rows of 4 blocks on point on your design wall or large flat surface. Fill in with 12 setting squares. Place the setting triangles and corner triangles in place.

2. Sew the blocks, setting squares, and setting triangles into diagonal rows. Press the seam allowances toward the blocks.

3. Sew the diagonal rows together, being careful to match the seam intersections. Press toward the bottom of the quilt.

4. Sew the 4 corner triangles to the quilt and press the seams toward the blocks.

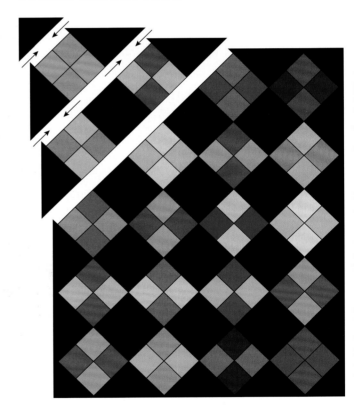

Quilt layout

5. Measure, cut, and sew the 1⅛″ blue-gray inner border strips to the pieced center. Sew the borders to the sides first, and then to the top and bottom (refer to Butted Borders, page 125).

6. Measure, cut, and sew the 2½″ outer border strips to the inner border, as in Step 5.

Quilting and Finishing

1. Mark quilting designs on the quilt top or plan to stitch without marking.

2. Layer and baste the quilt (see Layering and Basting in Quiltmaking Basics, page 123). Quilt by hand or machine.

3. Bind the quilt (see Binding in Quiltmaking Basics, page 123).

4. Make and attach a sleeve, if desired.

TIP

I hand quilted my quilt using purchased quilting stencils and a quilting motif. The quilting motif came from the book *Think Small: Over 300 Miniature Quilting Designs* by Shirley Thompson.

about the quiltmaker

Laura Mattox lives in Lynden, Washington, with her husband, Mike, and their Chihuahua, Lucy. They have two grown sons, Aaron and Matthew. Laura has been quilting for twenty years. Her first quilts were baby quilts made for each of her boys. Later she progressed to making the family's bed quilts. With so many patterns available, Laura soon learned that making smaller quilts to decorate the family home was her favorite pastime. Laura especially loves making doll-size quilts with simple patchwork and hand quilting. She draws her inspiration from looking at books with pictures of antique quilts; she loves to reproduce similar quilts that bring to mind the quilts of days gone by.

Besides quilting, Laura enjoys gardening, taking long walks, and making homemade soup in the crockpot for family and friends. Having something in the crockpot gives her more time to do what she loves—quilt!

amish square-within-a-square (bermuda)

FINISHED QUILT: 42½″ × 42½″

Made by Vicki Ayers Zoller

I love to hand quilt, so I am naturally drawn to the beauty of Amish quilts. I also like the strong graphic designs and colors that make Amish quilts so unique. As a beginning quilter many years ago, I was inspired by the David Pottinger collection of Amish quilts at the Indiana State Museum in Indianapolis. My guide in making my early quilts was Roberta Horton's *An Amish Adventure*. I felt as if I had a "Julie/Julia" relationship with Roberta for quite a while, because I made ten quilts from this wonderful book. This Square-within-a-Square quilt is a traditional Amish pattern that shows the juxtaposition of simple piecing and elaborate quilting that are hallmarks of Amish quilts. Although blue and pink can be traditional Amish color choices, my colors were inspired by the blue waters and pink sands of Bermuda, one of my favorite places.

MATERIALS

Black fabric: 1⅞ yards

Light pink fabric: ¼ yard

Medium blue fabric: ⅜ yard

Batting: 49″ × 49″

Backing fabric: 3 yards, or 1½ yards of 60″ or 90″-wide muslin

NOTE

60″ or 90″-wide muslin is suggested for the backing so that it does not have to be pieced. It is much easier to hand quilt (if desired) if the backing is one piece of fabric.

CUTTING

Black fabric

Refer to cutting diagram, at right.

Cut 1 square 16″ × 16″.

Cut 1 strip crosswise 2½″ × width of fabric. Subcut into 2 pieces 2½″ × 20″.

Cut 2 strips crosswise 2½″ × 24″.

Cut 5 strips crosswise 2¼″ × width of fabric for double-fold binding.

Cut 2 strips lengthwise 8″ × 28″.

Cut 2 strips lengthwise 8″ × 43″.

Light pink fabric

Cut 2 strips 2½″ × width of fabric. Subcut into 2 strips 2½″ × 16″ and 2 strips 2½″ × 20″.

Medium blue fabric

Cut 4 strips 2½″ × width of fabric. Subcut into 2 strips 2½″ × 24″ and 2 strips 2½″ × 28″.

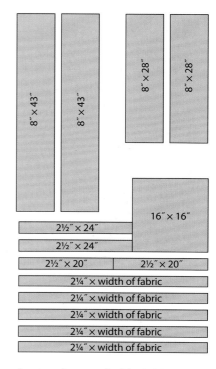

Cutting diagram for black fabric

construction

Press all seams toward the outside of the quilt.

Assembly

1. Sew 2½″ × 16″ light pink strips to each side of the black 16″ × 16″ square.

2. Sew 2½″ × 20″ light pink strips to the top and bottom of the black square.

3. Sew 2½″ × 20″ black strips to each side of the quilt.

4. Sew 2½″ × 24″ black strips to the top and bottom of the quilt.

5. Sew 2½″ × 24″ medium blue strips to each side of the quilt.

6. Sew 2½″ × 28″ medium blue strips to the top and bottom of the quilt.

7. Sew 8″ × 28″ borders to each side of the quilt.

8. Sew 8″ × 43″ borders to the top and bottom of the quilt.

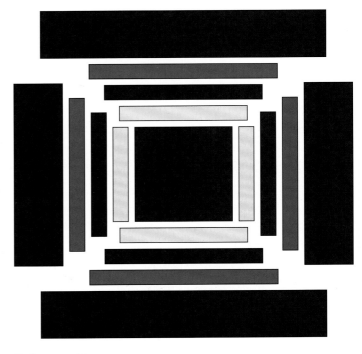

Quilt assembly

Quilting and Finishing

1. Mark quilting designs on the quilt top or plan to stitch without marking.

2. Layer and baste the quilt (see Layering and Basting in Quiltmaking Basics, page 123). Quilt by hand or machine.

3. Bind the quilt (see Binding in Quiltmaking Basics, page 123).

4. Make and attach a sleeve, if desired.

about the quiltmaker

Vicki Ayers Zoller has been quilting since 1981. She had been sewing for years but wanted to try the challenge of quilting, with an eye to displaying the quilts as a dramatic decorating treatment.

After teaching high school French and English for 27 years, she now pursues quilting full-time. She is active in her quilt guild in Jacksonville, Florida, and enjoys teaching classes, giving demonstrations, and creating and presenting programs. While she enjoys making quilts, fabric art journals, and fabric postcards, her true passion is hand quilting. She hand quilts all of her quilts. Several competition judges have noted her creative flair, strong use of color in design, and consistency of stitching. She has even been asked what machine she uses to produce her small, even stitches! Vicki has won numerous awards in local quilt shows and has done commissioned work.

amish schoolhouse

FINISHED BLOCK: 8″ × 8″ | **FINISHED QUILT:** 53″ × 53″

Made by Cathie Hoover

Amish quilts have delighted me ever since Roberta Horton's 1982 Amish quilts class at the Cotton Patch quilt shop in Lafayette, California. Once a week for twelve weeks, I journeyed 150 miles round trip to attend her class. It was delightful to work with solid colors and learn to assemble a number of different quilt blocks and quilts in the Amish palette. Roberta shared every bit and morsel of information she had gleaned from books about the Amish way of life and their religious choices. We studied photographs of Amish quilts from other books to get a sense of their color use, and we learned that the Amish always seemed to choose the easiest method of quilt construction. That certainly made emulating their quilts easier.

The Amish choice of quilting patterns was also a joy to follow. Simple shapes, repeated and interlocked, filled the solid blocks with beauty. The feathers, quilted to create both wreaths and swags, were formed from one's own thumb!

From my first view of the class sample hanging from the quilt shop's ceiling, I was hooked, and that attraction still exists today. I hope you allow yourself to be equally hooked on Amish quilts!

MATERIALS

Solid-color fabrics: A fat eighth* of each of a variety of 18 colors, and a small scrap (approximately 6″ × 6″) each of a variety of 8 colors, for the schoolhouse blocks

Black solid 1½ yards for sashing, inner border, and outer border

Magenta solid: ⅜ yard (¼ yard for middle border and balance for schoolhouse blocks)

Backing fabric: 3⅝ yards

Batting: 59″ × 59″ cotton batting

Binding: ½ yard solid magenta (a different value than what was used for inner border and schoolhouse blocks)

* Fat eighths measure approximately 9″ × 21″.

TOOLS

Template plastic: 1 large sheet

Permanent black marking pen, extra fine point

Push pin

Plastic baggies: 4 sandwich size

Blue painter's tape: any width

CUTTING

Black sashing

Cut 6 strips 2½″ × width of fabric. Subcut 4 rectangles 2½″ × 8½″ from each strip for a total of 24 sashing strips.

Black inner border

Cut 4 strips 2½″ × width of fabric.

Black outer border

Cut 5 strips 5″ × width of fabric.

Sashing squares

Cut 6 squares 2½″ × 2½″ from solid medium turquoise fabric.

Cut 3 squares 2½″ × 2½″ from solid medium purple fabric.

Magenta middle border

Cut 5 strips 1½″ × width of fabric.

Binding

Cut 6 strips 2½″ × width of fabric.

make the schoolhouse templates

Note: Each pattern has ¼″ seam allowance added. The dashed line on the patterns represents the seamline. The solid line represents the cutting line.

1. With a permanent marking pen and ruler, carefully trace each pattern piece (A–M2) onto the template plastic. Transfer all markings, including dashed lines, solid lines, registration dots (in every corner/angle), grain-lines, and identifying letters and numbers. Use blue tape to hold the plastic in place while tracing.

2. Cut out each of the 13 pattern templates, just along the *inside* of the traced line. This will add to the accuracy of your piecing!

3. Use a push pin to poke a hole in each template in the corners where you see a dot.

4. Place templates A, B, and C in a sandwich baggie labeled Row 1.

5. Place templates D, E, F, and G in a sandwich baggie labeled Row 2.

6. Place templates H, J, K1/K2, and L in a sandwich baggie labeled Section 1.

7. Place templates M1/M2 and I in a sandwich baggie labeled Section 2.

Tips for Using Templates

1. Refer to the quilt photo (page 53) when choosing colors for each block.

2. Trace each pattern piece on the *wrong* side of the selected fabric, *noting grainline markings and placing accordingly.* When cutting out each fabric shape, completely trim off the perimeter line. Doing so will add to the accuracy of your machine piecing!

3. See the block assembly diagrams for the number needed of each template per row or section. Note that in Row 1, you need 2 each of templates A and B and 1 of template C.

4. Mark the registration dots on the wrong side of each fabric piece, using a marker that contrasts clearly with the fabric.

construction

Block Assembly

1. The following tips apply to all the pieces within the Schoolhouse block:

- Increase accuracy by pinning the registration dots in the top fabric to the registration dots in the lower fabric.

- Press all seam allowances in alternate directions from Row 1 to Row 2.

- Verify that you are sewing with an accurate ¼″ seam to ensure that your blocks will finish to 8″ × 8″.

2. Start block assembly with Row 1 of your first schoolhouse. Sew 2 units of AB shapes, and then sew the B side of each unit to either end of C.

Assembled Row 1

3. Row 2 has several triangles and other shapes with diagonal sides. It is especially important to match registration dots on these shapes. Work from left to right, pressing seams in the opposite direction from Row 1.

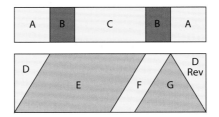

Assembled Rows 1 and 2

NOTE

I reversed the Schoolhouse when I pieced my personal block for this quilt. (It's in the bottom row, second from the right.) If you want to do this, simply flip each template and use the mirror image.

4. After piecing Rows 1 and 2, sew them together, matching registration dots along this new seamline. The top unit is now complete.

5. Piece lower Section 1 and lower Section 2. Press open.

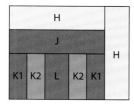 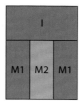

Assembled lower Section 1   Assembled lower Section 2

6. Sew lower Sections 1 and 2 together, pressing open. The lower unit is now complete.

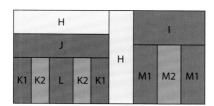

Completed lower section

7. Sew the top unit to the lower unit.

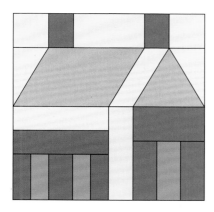

Completed block

8. Congratulations! Continue to piece each of the remaining 15 blocks.

9. Arrange the blocks in an order that pleases you, using the setting shown in the original photograph (page 53): 4 rows of 4 blocks each.

Make Sashing and Corner Squares

1. Sew 3 sashing strips 2½″ × 8½″ to 4 Schoolhouse blocks, as shown in the Schoolhouse row assembly diagram. Press seam allowances toward the sashing strips. Make 4 rows.

Schoolhouse row assembly—make 4 rows.

2. Sew 9 cornerstones 2½″ × 2½″ to each of 9 black sashing strips 2½″ × 8½. Make 6 with the blue-green squares and 3 with the purple squares. Press the seam allowances toward the sashing strips.

Make 6 black/blue-green and 3 black/purple.

3. Sew 2 rows of sashing using the black strips with blue-green cornerstones. Sew 1 row of sashing using the black strips with purple cornerstones.

Make 2 black/blue-green and 1 black/purple.

4. Sew sashing/cornerstone units to the bottom edge of a row of blocks. Make 3.

Schoolhouse blocks and horizontal sashing

5. Sew all 4 rows together, as shown in the quilt assembly diagram (page 59).

Borders

Black Inner Border

1. Sew 2½″ × width of fabric strips end-to-end to make 1 long strip. Cut into 2 strips 2½″ × 38½″ and 2 strips 2½″ × 42½″.

2. Sew 1 black strip 2½″ × 38½″ to each side of the quilt. Press seams toward the borders.

3. Sew 1 black strip 2½″ × 42½″ to the top and bottom edges of quilt. Press seams toward the borders.

Magenta Middle Border

1. Sew 1½″ × width of fabric strips end-to-end to make one long strip. Cut into 2 strips 1½″ × 42½″ and 2 strips 1½″ × 44½″.

2. Sew 1 magenta strip 1½″ × 42½″ to each side of quilt. Press seams toward the quilt's outer edge.

3. Sew 1 magenta strip 1½″ × 44½″ to the quilt's top and bottom edges. Press seams toward the quilt's outer edge.

Black Outer Border

1. Sew 5″ × width of fabric strips end-to-end to make 1 long strip. Cut into 2 strips 5″ × 44½″ and 2 strips 5″ × 53½″.

2. Sew 1 black strip 5″ × 44½″ to each side of quilt. Press seams toward the quilt's outer edge.

3. Sew 1 black strip 5″ × 53½″ to the top and bottom edges of quilt. Press seams toward the quilt's outer edge.

Quilt assembly

Quilting and Finishing

1. Mark quilting designs on the quilt top or plan to stitch without marking.

2. Layer and baste the quilt (see Layering and Basting in Quiltmaking Basics, page 123). Quilt by hand or machine.

3. Bind the quilt (see Binding in Quiltmaking Basics, page 123).

4. Make and attach a sleeve, if desired.

NOTE

If you plan to embroider names or details, do so before layering and basting. Be sure to use an embroidery hoop, and do not pull your stitches too tight!

about the quiltmaker

Cathie Hoover is a third-generation Californian and a Napa High School graduate. She earned her bachelor of science degree in home economics from Chico State College. She has been sewing since she was a child and quilting since 1979. In 1988, she began teaching quilting, as well as judging quilts and wearable art.

Cathie's ten-year experience as the West Coast field editor for *American Quilter* magazine added extensive knowledge and innovative techniques to her skill base.

Her chosen art medium is fabric. Within its wide design possibilities, she has found everything necessary to express her creativity. Her participation in multiple Fairfield/Bernina fashion shows has provided a venue to express her love of quilting in "wearable, quilt-based" clothing. However, Cathie continues to create original wall quilts that combine skilled piecework and machine appliqué.

Color is of utmost importance to her, and she uses bright, bold chunks of color in her quilt art. Rickrack and other trims, polka dots, stripes, florals, and geometric prints are all about the color and movement Cathie uses in her art.

TEMPLATE PATTERNS FOR *AMISH SCHOOLHOUSE*

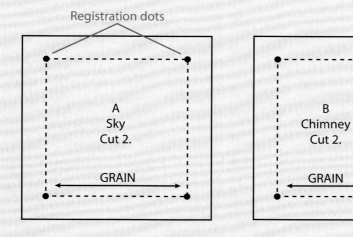

Registration dots

A
Sky
Cut 2.

GRAIN

B
Chimney
Cut 2.

GRAIN

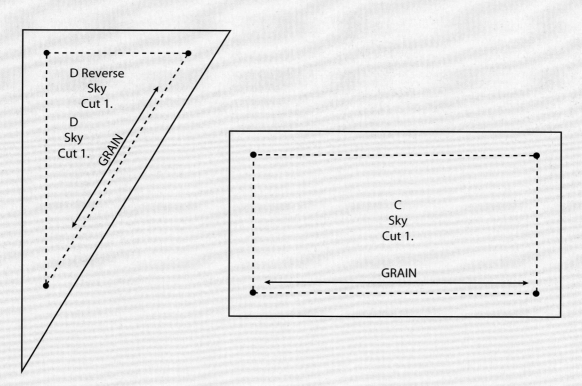

D Reverse
Sky
Cut 1.

D
Sky
Cut 1.

GRAIN

C
Sky
Cut 1.

GRAIN

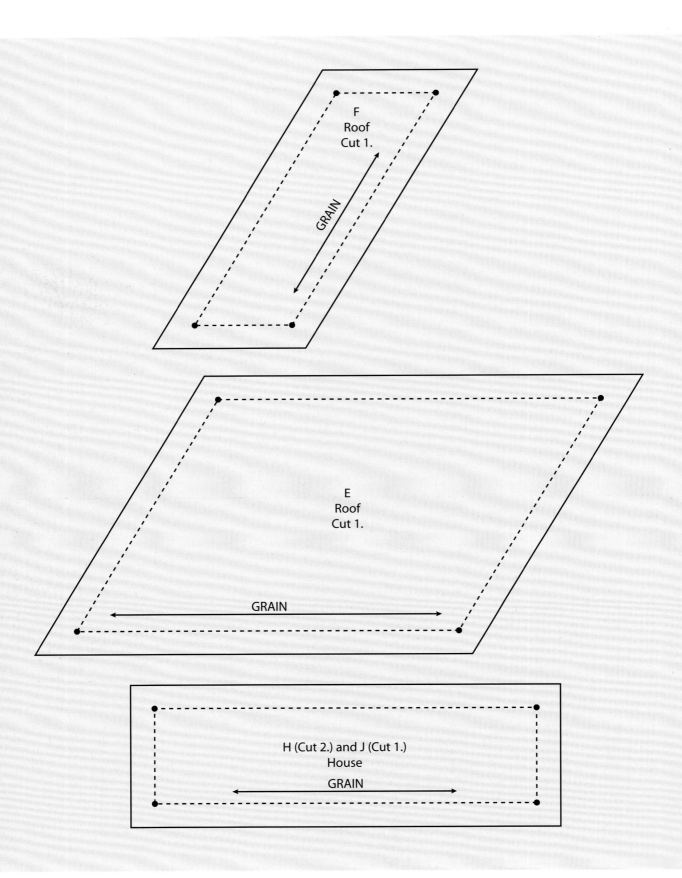

F
Roof
Cut 1.

GRAIN

E
Roof
Cut 1.

GRAIN

H (Cut 2.) and J (Cut 1.)
House
GRAIN

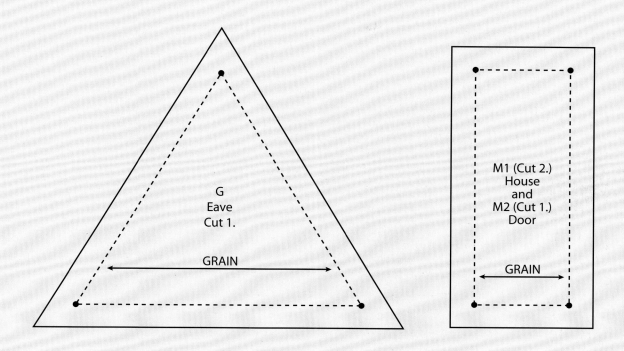

G
Eave
Cut 1.

GRAIN

M1 (Cut 2.)
House
and
M2 (Cut 1.)
Door

GRAIN

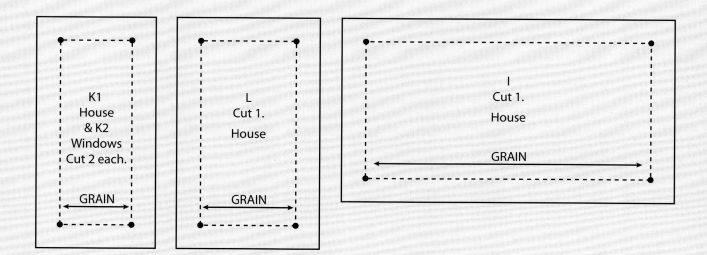

K1
House
& K2
Windows
Cut 2 each.

GRAIN

L
Cut 1.
House

GRAIN

I
Cut 1.
House

GRAIN

streak of lightning

FINISHED BLOCK: 6⅜″ × 6⅜″ | **FINISHED QUILT:** 19¾″ × 38⅞″

Made by Susan Galloway Hilsenbeck

I took a class from Roberta Horton sometime between 1983 (when my signed copy of Horton's *An Amish Adventure* was published) and 1986 (when I made this quilt). It was a life-altering experience. I went on an Amish kick and made a number of small pieces. I absolutely love the simplicity and the way blocks and geometric design stand out from the dark background (although hand quilting with black thread on a black background is really hard on the eyes!). The style of the quilts and the solid-color fabrics featured in Horton's book are traditional, yet surprisingly contemporary. Even after many years of quilting in different styles, I find myself returning to this aesthetic.

This quilt was made during an especially rough time of my life, and it is the only one I did not give away. It hangs in my office at Baylor College of Medicine, where I enjoy it every day. My colleagues think it looks like DNA, so they think it is very modern. The design is my own but is based on Lesson 2–Roman Stripes from Horton's book. It is also a small variation on her Exercise #4–Chevron Roman Stripe.

MATERIALS

Streak fabrics: A variety of green, teal, and gray-green solid fabrics (or other analogous mixture of muted and bright Amish shades) to make 12 strips 1¼˝ wide, each at least 35˝ long. Use related shades that will carry the eye through the entire "streak," alternating darker and lighter shades and with one brighter fabric to add some sparkle.

Dark or black fabric: ⅞ yard for background

Middle accent border: ⅛ yard, similar to streak fabrics

Backing fabric: 1⅜ yards

Batting: 26˝ × 45˝

Binding fabric: ½ yard solid fabric similar to streak fabrics

Cardstock or template plastic: 7¼˝ × 7¼˝

CUTTING

Streak fabrics

Cut 12 strips 1¼″ × 35″.

Background fabric

Note: Measurements assume that completed streak strip sets measure 5″ wide.

Cut 3 strips 1½″ × width of fabric for inner background border.

Cut 3 strips 2½″ × width of fabric for outer background border.

Cut 5 squares 7¼″ × 7¼″. Cut on the diagonal once for 10 half-square triangles.

Middle accent border fabric

Cut 3 strips 1″ × width of fabric for accent border.

Binding fabric

Cut 4 strips 3⅛″ × width of fabric for double-fold binding that will finish ½″ wide.

TIP

Make the quilt modern by using a light background. Mix prints and solids in coordinating modern colors for the streak, accent border, and binding fabrics.

construction

Make Streak Strip Sets

1. Select 6 streak strips. Sew alternating lighter and darker strips together to make a strip set measuring 5″ × 35″.

2. Repeat Step 1 with the remaining 6 strips, but place the colors in a different order. Throw in a clear, light value to add sparkle.

3. Make a triangle template from the cardstock or template plastic by first accurately drawing a 7¼″ × 7¼″ square. Then cut it once on the diagonal.

4. Carefully mark cutting lines on the streak strip sets, rotating the template. Cut on the lines with a rotary ruler and cutter *or* temporarily affix the template to a corner of the underside of a square rotary ruler. Use it to cut by aligning the base of the triangle with the edge of the fabric. You will get 3 A triangles and 2 B triangles from each 35″-long streak strip set, for a total of 10 triangles.

NOTE

Align the base (long side) of the triangle on the fabric's edge. The tip of the triangle will extend approximately ⅛″ off the fabric on the other side.

Cut streak triangles.

Block Assembly

1. Sew a background triangle to each strip triangle to make 10 blocks. Press toward the dark fabric.

NOTE

The outer edge of the streak part of the block is on the bias. Exercise care when handling, pressing, and sewing to avoid distortion.

Streak block

Quilt Assembly

Quilt Center

1. Arrange the blocks on a design wall or large flat surface.

TIP

If desired, gently re-press seams to change the direction and reduce bulk when sewing.

2. Sew the blocks together. Press seams in alternate directions.

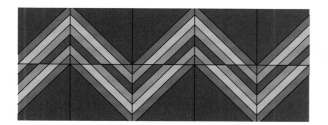

Quilt center

Borders

1. Sew 3 inner background border strips together end-to-end. Measure, cut, and sew inner background strips to the quilt center. Press seams away from the center (refer to Butted Borders in Quiltmaking Basics, page 123).

2. Repeat Step 1 for the middle accent border and the outer background border. Press seams away from the center.

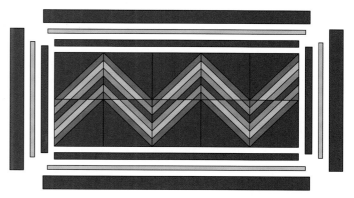

Quilt assembly

Quilting and Finishing

1. Mark quilting designs on the quilt top or plan to stitch without marking.

2. Layer and baste the quilt (see Layering and Basting in Quiltmaking Basics, page 123). Quilt by hand or machine.

3. Bind the quilt using a ½″ seam allowance (see Binding in Quiltmaking Basics, page 123).

4. Make and attach a sleeve, if desired.

about the quiltmaker

Susan Hilsenbeck is a biostatistician and professor of medicine at Baylor College of Medicine in Houston, Texas. She has been a quilter for 30 years. Early in her career, she took Roberta Horton's class on Amish quilts and was inspired to make a number of small, Amish-style wall quilts. Many of them were based on variations of this Streak of Lightning design, and nearly all were given away to colleagues and friends. After a hiatus from quilting of nearly ten years, Susan came back to quilting in 2000, first designing and organizing group quilts for coworkers to commemorate important life events, and then, more recently, to explore a personal artistic vision. Susan is still an avid class taker who is always eager to learn. She has also started collecting small art quilts. To her, quilting is the perfect blend of artistic expression, precise engineering, and skilled construction.

baskets—cake stand

FINISHED BLOCK: 5″ × 5″ | **FINISHED QUILT:** 33″ × 33″

Made by Veronica Haberthuer

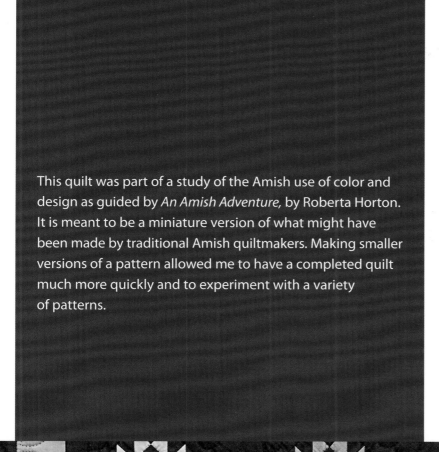

This quilt was part of a study of the Amish use of color and design as guided by *An Amish Adventure,* by Roberta Horton. It is meant to be a miniature version of what might have been made by traditional Amish quiltmakers. Making smaller versions of a pattern allowed me to have a completed quilt much more quickly and to experiment with a variety of patterns.

MATERIALS

Solid-color fabrics: ⅛ yard each of 9 different colors for baskets

Light turquoise fabric: ⅜ yard for inner border

Black fabric: 2¾ yards for setting, backing, and binding

Batting: 39″ × 39″

CUTTING

Solid-color fabric for baskets

Cut 4 squares 1⅞″ × 1⅞″ from each color.

Cut 1 square 3⅞″ × 3⅞″ from each color. Cut diagonally once to yield 2 triangles (only 1 will be used).

Light turquoise fabric for inner border

Cut 2 strips 2½″ × 25½″.

Cut 2 strips 2½″ × 21½″.

Black fabric

Cut 4 squares 1⅞″ × 1⅞″ for each basket. Cut a total of 36.

Cut 5 squares 3⅞″ × 3⅞″. Cut diagonally once to make 10 triangles, 1 for each basket (only 9 will be used).

Cut 2 squares 1½″ × 1½″ for each basket. Cut a total of 18.

Cut 2 rectangles 1½″ × 3½″ for each basket. Cut a total of 18.

Cut 4 squares 5½″ × 5½″ for setting the blocks.

Cut 2 squares 8¼″ × 8¼″. Cut each on the diagonal twice to create 8 triangles for setting the blocks.

Cut 2 squares 4½″ × 4½″. Cut on the diagonal once to create 4 triangles for the corners.

Cut 2 strips 4½″ × 33½″.

Cut 2 strips 4½″ × 25½″.

Cut 4 strips 2½″ × width of fabric for binding.

Save remainder for the backing.

construction

TIPS

- Press all seams toward black fabric.
- Trim triangle points after sewing seams.
- After sewing and pressing each seam, place pieces into the design to make sure you are sewing them in the right position.

Completed block

Half-Square Triangles

1. Make half-square triangles by placing each color 1⅞″ × 1⅞″ square on top of a black 1⅞″ × 1⅞″ square, with right sides together.

2. Draw a line diagonally across the square with a pencil.

3. Sew a ¼″ seam on each side of the drawn line.

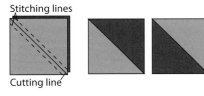

Make 8 (from 4 sets of squares).

4. Cut along the drawn line.

5. Open and press.

6. Repeat Steps 1–5 to make 8 half-square triangle units per color.

7. Repeat Steps 1–6 for each color (1 color per basket).

Block Assembly

1. Arrange the pieces of the basket squares to match the design.

2. Sew 3 of the half-square triangle units together. Press. Make 2.

3. Sew the color and black triangles (created from the 3⅞″ × 3⅞″ squares) together. Press.

4. Sew 1 strip of 3 pieced squares to the black half of the half-square triangle unit from Step 3.

5. Sew the other strip of pieced squares to a 1½″ × 1½″ black square. Press.

6. Sew the strip from Step 5 to the other side of the large half-square triangle unit. Press.

7. Sew a small half-square triangle unit to one end of a black 1½″ × 3½″ rectangle. Press. Repeat to make a second one reversing the orientation of the half-square triangle unit.

8. Sew a strip from Step 7 to the color side of the large half-square triangle unit.

9. Sew a black 1½″ × 1½″ square to the pieced end of the remaining strip from Step 7. Press.

10. Sew the strip from Step 9 to the other color side of the large half-square triangle unit. Press.

11. Repeat Steps 1–10 for each basket block.

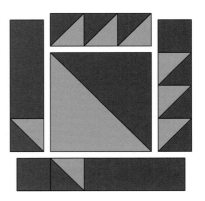

Block assembly

Quilt Assembly

1. Arrange the blocks and setting pieces.

2. Sew the blocks and pieces in diagonal rows. Press.

3. Sew the diagonal rows together, matching block corners and easing fabrics to match. Press.

4. Sew the 2½″ × 21½″ turquoise inner border strips to the sides of the quilt. Press.

5. Sew the 2½″ × 25½″ turquoise inner border strips to the top and bottom of the quilt. Press.

6. Sew the 4½″ × 25½″ black outer border strips to the sides of the quilt. Press.

7. Sew the 4½″ × 33½″ black outer border strips to the top and bottom of the quilt. Press.

about the quiltmaker

Veronica Haberthuer has been quilting since 1976. Her quilts have won the Juror's Choice Award in Alaska's Earth, Fire, and Fibre show and have been juried into Quilt San Diego's Visions: QuiltArt.

Quilt assembly

Quilting and Finishing

1. Mark quilting designs on the quilt top or plan to stitch without marking.

2. Layer and baste the quilt (see Layering and Basting in Quiltmaking Basics, page 123). Quilt by hand or machine.

3. Bind the quilt (see Binding in Quiltmaking Basics, page 123).

4. Make and attach a sleeve, if desired.

double nine-patch

FINISHED BLOCK: 11¼″ × 11¼″ | **FINISHED QUILT:** 75½″ × 75½″

Made by Veronica Haberthuer

After working in traditional designs for many years, I studied Amish color and design by following the lessons in Roberta Horton's *An Amish Adventure*. The choices in fabric design available to quilters today can be overwhelming and can even stunt creativity. The beauty of traditional Amish quilts attests to the value of limiting choices, either through edict or choice. Similar to a photographer or an artist working in black and white, I have found that imposing limitations is a valuable tool for developing artistic expression.

MATERIALS

Bright turquoise fabric: 7¾ yards for outer borders, half-square setting triangles, backing*, and binding

Black fabric: 1⅓ yards for inner borders and outer border corner squares

Grayed turquoise fabric: ⅞ yards for large setting squares and corner triangles

Light turquoise fabric: ⅝ yard for Nine-Patch setting blocks

Solid-color fabric scraps: A variety of 15–20 colors to make 49 small Nine-Patch blocks (You will need less than ⅛ yard of each color.)

Batting: 82″ × 82″

* Backing fabric must be at least 42″ wide.

CUTTING

Bright turquoise fabric

Cut 6 strips 10½″ × width of fabric for outer border.

Cut 2 squares 17¼″ × 17¼″. Cut diagonally twice for 8 setting triangles.

Black fabric

Cut 5 strips 4¼″ × width of fabric for inner border.

Cut 4 squares 10½″ × 10½″ for outer border corner blocks.

Grayed turquoise fabric

Cut 4 squares 11¾″ × 11¾″ for setting squares.

Cut 2 squares 8⅞″ × 8⅞″. Cut diagonally once for 4 corner triangles.

Light turquoise fabric

Cut 36 squares 4¼″ × 4¼″ for setting the small Nine-Patches.

Solid-color fabric scraps

Cut 4 squares 1¾″ × 1¾″ of one color and 5 squares 1¾″ × 1¾″ of another color for each small Nine-Patch square. You will need enough combinations to make 49 small Nine-Patches.

Backing and binding

Cut 2 pieces 82″ × width of fabric from the bright turquoise fabric. Trim off the selvage from one side of each piece. Sew the trimmed sides together lengthwise with a ¼″ seam. Press to one side.

Cut 9 strips 2½″ × width of fabric from the bright turquoise fabric for binding.

construction

Seam allowances are ¼".

TIPS

- Pin carefully and ease fabrics as needed.
- Press all seams toward the black fabric.
- Trim triangle points after sewing and pressing seams.

Double Nine-Patch Block Assembly

1. Sew together 3 squares 1¾" × 1¾" to make a row. Mix light colors with medium or dark colors to create contrast. Make 3 rows. Press.

2. Sew the 3 rows from Step 1 together to make a small Nine-Patch block. Press. The block will measure 4¼" × 4¼" square, including seam allowances.

3. Repeat Steps 1 and 2 to make 49 small Nine-Patch blocks.

Make 49.

4. Sew a small Nine-Patch block, light turquoise square, and another small Nine-Patch together. Press. Make 2.

5. Sew a light turquoise square, small Nine-Patch, and another light turquoise square together. Press.

6. Join the 3 rows from Steps 4 and 5 together to make a double Nine-Patch square.

7. Repeat Steps 4–6 to make 9 double Nine-Patch squares. You will have 4 small Nine-Patch squares left over for the inner border corners.

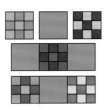

Make 9.

8. Arrange the double Nine-Patch squares with the setting squares, setting triangles, and corner triangles.

9. Sew the double Nine-Patch squares and setting pieces together in diagonal rows. Press.

10. Sew the diagonal rows together, making sure to pin carefully to match corners. Press.

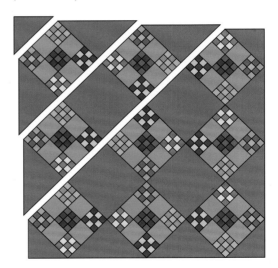

Double Nine-Patch assembly

Borders

1. Sew the black 4¼" border strips together end-to-end. Cut 4 strips 4¼" × 48½".

2. Sew a remaining small Nine-Patch square to each end of a black 4¼" × 48½" inner border strip. Press. Make 2.

3. Sew a 4¼" × 48½" black inner border to the top and bottom of the double Nine-Patch center. Press.

4. Sew the black inner borders with the 2 Nine-Patch squares on the ends (from Step 2) to the sides of the double Nine-Patch center. Press.

5. Sew the bright turquoise 10½" outer border strips together end-to-end. Cut 4 strips 10½" × 56".

6. Sew 2 bright turquoise outer border strips to the top and bottom of the inner border. Press.

7. Sew a 10½" × 10½" black square to each end of the remaining bright turquoise outer border strips. Press.

8. Sew the bright turquoise outer border strips with the black squares to the sides of the inner border. Press.

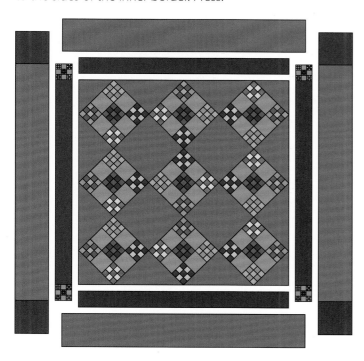

Quilt assembly

Quilting and Finishing

1. Mark quilting designs on the quilt top or plan to stitch without marking.

2. Layer and baste the quilt (see Layering and Basting in Quiltmaking Basics, page 123). Quilt by hand or machine.

3. Bind the quilt (see Binding in Quiltmaking Basics, page 123).

4. Make and attach a sleeve, if desired.

about the quiltmaker

Veronica Haberthuer has been quilting since 1976. Her quilts have won the Juror's Choice Award in Alaska's Earth, Fire, and Fibre show and have been juried into Quilt San Diego's Visions: QuiltArt.

amish sunshine and shadow diamond-in-a-square

FINISHED QUILT: 51¾″ × 51¾″

Made by Ellen Dambacher

My first quilts were made for my children in the early 1970s, when few people were quilting. Rotary cutters, cutting boards, and plastic rulers were unknown. Relying on basic sewing skills, I made appliquéd quilts as each child arrived. Amish quilts were far from my mind.

When quilting became popular in the 1990s and I joined my first guild, I was drawn to the simple geometric designs and beautiful colors of Amish quilts. While others were purchasing the latest print fabrics, I was already drawn to solid colors.

When I saw my first book on Amish quilts, I was happy to learn that beautiful quilts can be made with solid colors! It was love at first sight. Inspired by the beautiful quilts before me, my first Amish quilt was quickly drafted, sewn, and hand quilted. Within the year, I had made a king-size Diamond-in-a-Square quilt for my nephew and his bride.

I never grow tired of browsing through Amish quilt books. The simplicity, range of colors, and exquisite hand quilting draw me to them. I could make every quilt featured within the pages and never grow weary. Their hand-quilted designs have inspired me to hand quilt all of my quilts. Yes, I do make quilts using printed fabrics, but an Amish quilt is always waiting to come to life.

MATERIALS

Bright yellow fabric: 2″ × 2″ scrap

Chartreuse fabric: ¼ yard

Purple fabric: ⅛ yard

Dark rose fabric: ⅛ yard

Cranberry fabric: ⅛ yard

Pink fabric: ⅛ yard

Blue fabric: ¼ yard

Periwinkle fabric: ¼ yard

Black fabric: ⅞ yard

Bright green fabric: ¼ yard

Burgundy fabric: ⅝ yard

Dark green fabric: 1½ yards

Backing fabric: 3½ yards

Batting: 58″ × 58″

Fabric notes:

Amish Sunshine and Shadow began as a study in color when I took Gai Perry's class on color. In her class, I learned how to apply what I see around me to the colors I choose for my quilts. We were encouraged to use fabrics from our stash, so I brought my largest stash—my solids.

If you choose to select your own color scheme, remember that you want to create visual movement back and forth between lights and darks, or warm and cool colors, in your sunshine and shadows portion. Adding light, medium, and dark values of a color will give your quilt a shimmering quality. Placing your darkest color in the #9 position will define the diamond and frame the inside of your Sunshine and Shadows. You may also want to repeat a color.

Before cutting into your fabric, place your choices side by side in the order that they will be placed to make sure your colors flow together. You should also make sure that there is enough contrast to make your quilt interesting. Audition fabrics for your setting triangles and borders, ensuring that they complement your color choices for the Sunshine and Shadow Diamond.

CUTTING

Bright yellow fabric

Cut 1 square 2″ × 2″ for center position.

Chartreuse fabric

Cut 2 strips 2″ × width of fabric. Subcut into 40 squares 2″ × 2″—4 for Round 1 and 36 for Round 9 of the diamond.

Purple fabric

Cut 1 strip 2″ × width of fabric. Subcut into 8 squares 2″ × 2″ for Round 2 of the diamond.

Dark rose fabric

Cut 1 strip 2″ × width of fabric. Subcut into 12 squares 2″ × 2″ for Round 3 of the diamond.

Cranberry fabric

Cut 1 strip 2″ × width of fabric. Subcut into 16 squares 2″ × 2″ for Round 4 of the diamond.

Pink fabric

Cut 1 strip 2″ × width of fabric. Subcut into 20 squares 2″ × 2″ for Round 5 of the diamond.

Blue fabric

Cut 2 strips 2″ × width of fabric. Subcut into 24 squares 2″ × 2″ for Round 6 of the diamond.

Periwinkle fabric

Cut 2 strips 2″ × width of fabric. Subcut into 28 squares 2″ × 2″ for Round 7 of the diamond.

Black fabric

Cut 2 strips 2″ × width of fabric. Subcut into 32 squares 2″ × 2″ for Round 8 of the diamond. Cut 4 strips 2½″ × 28″ for inner border. Cut 4 squares 8½″ × 8½″ for border corner squares.

Bright green fabric

Cut 1 strip 3⅜″ × width of fabric. Subcut into 9 squares 3⅜″ × 3⅜″. Then cut diagonally twice for 36 setting triangles.

Cut 2 squares 1⅞″ × 1⅞″. Then cut diagonally once for 4 corner triangles.

Burgundy fabric

Cut 2 squares 20″ × 20″. Subcut squares diagonally once for 4 corner triangles. (This cut is best left until just before you are adding the triangles to the Sunshine and Shadow diamond unit.)

Dark green fabric

Cut 4 lengthwise strips 8½″ × 38″ for outside border. Cut 5 strips 2½″ × width of fabric for double-fold binding.

NOTE

Because ¼″ seam allowances often vary, the two border lengths have been lengthened, and the squares for the burgundy corner triangles have been oversized to allow for any needed cutting adjustments.

construction

Sunshine and Shadow Mock-up

1. Place the bright yellow square in the middle of your design board. Arrange 4 of the chartreuse squares around it. This is Round 1. Continue placing squares, working out in color order until you have 9 rounds. The last round of squares is chartreuse (repeated from Round 1).

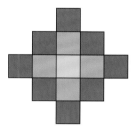

2. Place a bright green setting triangle at the end of each row with the bias edge against the square. Place the 4 corner triangles at each corner with the bias edge against the square.

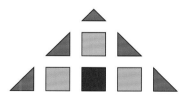

NOTE

If you are using your own color selection, check the placement of colors. Do you have enough play between darks and lights? Is there good value change? Make sure the colors you have chosen for the borders and large corner triangles complement the Sunshine and Shadow diamond. Do you like what you see? If not, now is the time for changes.

Assembly

NOTE

Press seams in the direction indicated in the text or diagrams. Press each seam when sewn. Make sure the unit is flat and seams are facing in the correct direction. Using a clear starch alternative spray when pressing and allowing the fabric to cool before moving keeps the unit flat and ready for the next seam.

Sunshine and Shadow

Keep the mock-up on your design board and remove each row to be sewn in turn. This provides you with a visual of the diamond and enables you to catch any construction mistakes.

1. Remove the top corner triangle and first row from your mock-up. Sew a setting triangle to one side of the square, right sides together and bias edge toward the square. Sew the second setting triangle to the opposite side of the square, right sides together and bias edge toward the square. Press seams to the left.

First row of diamond

2. Sew the top corner triangle, right sides together and bias edge toward the top of the square, making sure the point of the triangle lines up with the mid-point of the side of the square. Press this seam allowance downward. This unit becomes the top of your diamond.

Align centers.   Top of diamond

3. Remove Row 2 from your mock-up. Sew a setting triangle to a side of the first square. Continue sewing squares in order, ending with the second setting triangle. Press. Repeat for Rows 3–9, pressing seams in alternate directions from row to row.

4. Row 10 has corner triangles instead of setting triangles at the beginning and end of the row. Sew the bias edge of a corner triangle to the side of a square. Make sure the triangle's point lines up with the mid-point of the side of the square. Continue sewing squares in order, ending with the second corner triangle. Press.

Row 10

5. Continue sewing Rows 11–18 in the same way as Rows 2–9, except that now the setting triangles face downward. Press seams in alternating directions from row to row.

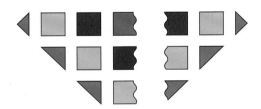

6. Sew the 19th row in the same manner as the first row. This time, however, the corner triangle is sewn to the bottom of the square.

Row 19—the last row

7. Rows are now ready to be sewn together. Check that seams have been pressed in alternating directions from row to row. Sew Rows 1 and 2 together, right sides together, placing pins at seam intersections to hold fabrics in place. (When correctly sewn and pressed, seams will meet and nestle together at each intersection.) After sewing, check for accuracy, and then press the seam downward. Continue sewing rows together in this manner until the diamond is complete.

Inner Border

1. Measure all 4 sides of the unfinished Sunshine and Shadow Diamond unit. Determine the average length. Cut 2 of the 2½″ × 28″ black inner border strips to match that length. Sew the strips to opposite sides of the diamond unit, right sides together. Press seams toward the black border.

2. Measure across the diamond and borders, at both ends and the middle. Determine an average measurement. Cut the remaining 2 black inner border strips to match. Sew strips to the remaining sides of the diamond, pressing seams toward the black border.

Corner Triangles

1. Sew the bias edge of an oversized burgundy corner triangle to one side of the center diamond unit, right sides together, making sure the triangle is pointing directly to the middle of the diamond. Press the seam toward the inner border.

2. Sew a second burgundy triangle to the opposite side of the diamond unit, making sure the triangle is pointing directly to the middle of the diamond unit. Continue with the remaining 2 corner triangles, pressing each seam in turn toward the inner black border.

3. Trim the oversized burgundy triangles, leaving a ¼″ seam allowance outside the black border.

Borders

1. Measure the outside edges of the center diamond and square unit to determine an average length for your borders. Then trim 4 dark green 8½″ × 38″ strips to match this measurement.

2. Sew 2 border strips to opposite sides of the quilt top, easing in any fabric as needed. Press the seams toward the dark green border.

3. Sew a black 8½″ × 8½″ square to each end of the remaining border strips. Press seams toward the dark green border strips.

4. Sew each of the dark green and black corner square borders to the 2 remaining sides of the quilt top. Match corner square seams to the border seam, placing pins as needed to ease fabric. Press the seam toward the dark green border.

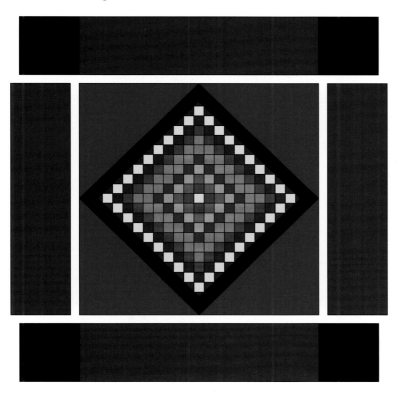

Quilt assembly

Backing

Cut the backing fabric into 2 pieces, each 58″ × width of fabric. Remove selvages on the seam edges. Sew the 2 pieces together lengthwise and press the seam open.

Quilting and Finishing

1. Mark quilting designs on the quilt top or plan to stitch without marking.

2. Layer and baste the quilt (see Layering and Basting in Quiltmaking Basics, page 123). Quilt by hand or machine.

3. Bind the quilt (see Binding in Quiltmaking Basics, page 123).

4. Make and attach a sleeve, if desired.

about the quiltmaker

Known for her Amish-style quilts, Ellen Dambacher has been quilting since the early 1990s, when she made her first quilt, a Diamond-in-a-Square. Drawn to the beauty and the simple geometric designs of the Amish, her favorite quilts are from this genre. In 2006, Ellen was asked by Anelie Belden to make a quilt for her book *Thoroughly Modern Dresden*.

Several of Ellen's quilts have won ribbons at the California State Fair, and she was honored to be her guild's Featured Quilter in 2011. Ellen enjoys all styles of quiltmaking, but Amish is always her favorite.

amish nine-patch

FINISHED QUILT: 37½″ × 37½″

Made by Annette Anderson

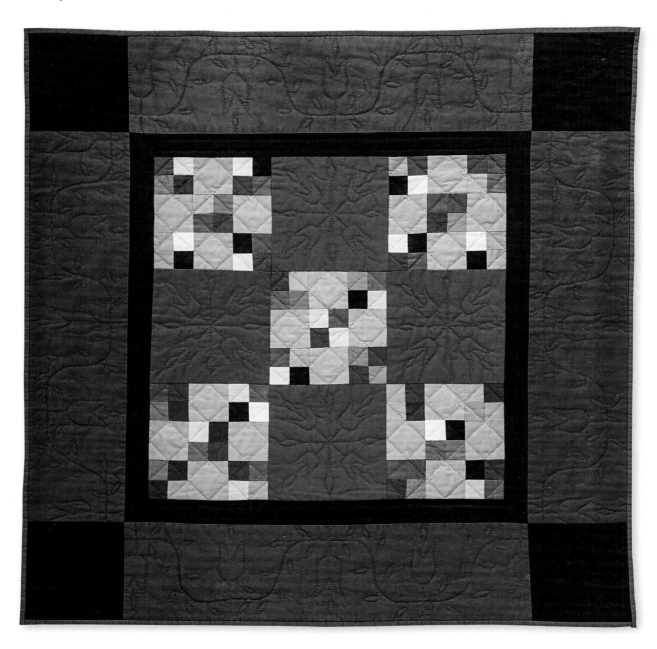

I was first inspired by Amish quilts because of their graphic impact and bold colors. The stark simplicity of design has always been aesthetically appealing to me. The Amish women have taken their limitations of pattern to an extreme art form by their controlled use of color. The manipulation of limited colors, bold or muted, expresses their individuality and genius.

I can play forever, putting one fabric next to another and observing how each color affects the other in its value and intensity. This realization has continued to have a great influence on my quiltmaking, as my favorite part of making a quilt is choosing the fabrics for each project. It is, and continues to be, about the fabric!

As a modern quiltmaker, I find that the graphic elements and limitations of the Amish designs have influenced how I view and appreciate the use of spatial design and line in Japanese art and architecture.

MATERIALS

Assorted light, medium, and dark solid fabrics: A variety to total about ⅓ yard for Four-Patch blocks

Light blue-green fabric: ¼ yard for Nine-Patch blocks

Dark teal fabric: ¼ yard for large squares

Black fabric: ⅓ yard for inner border

Navy blue fabric: ¼ yard for corner squares

Dark purple fabric: 1⅜ yards for outer borders and binding

Batting: 44″ × 44″

Backing fabric*: 1¼ yards

* Backing fabric must be at least 44″ wide.

cutting and construction

Seam allowances are ¼".

Four-Patch Block Assembly

1. Cut 100 squares 1¾" × 1¾" of light, medium, and dark.

2. Sew 25 Four-Patch blocks. Four-Patch blocks should measure 3" × 3".

Make 25.

Nine-Patch Block Assembly

1. Cut 20 squares 3" × 3" of light blue-green.

2. Sew 5 Nine-Patch blocks using 5 of the Four-Patch blocks and 4 light blue-green squares for each Nine-Patch. The block should measure 8" × 8".

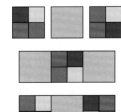

Make 5.

Nine-Patch Inner Section Assembly

1. Cut 4 dark teal squares 8" × 8".

2. Sew the large Nine-Patch center, using the 5 small Nine-Patch blocks and the 4 dark teal squares. The large Nine-Patch section should measure 23" × 23" after sewing.

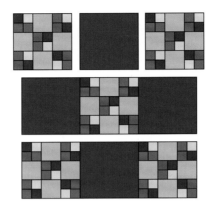

Black Inner Border

1. Cut 2 black borders 2" × 23". Sew these to the top and bottom of the Nine-Patch center.

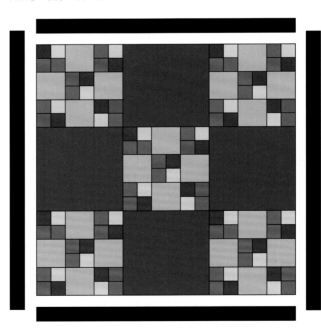

2. Cut 2 black borders 2" × 26". Sew these to the remaining sides of the Nine-Patch center. The center section with borders should now measure 26" × 26" square.

Dark Purple Outer Border with Corner Squares

1. Cut 4 pieces 6½″ × 26″ from dark purple fabric.

2. Cut 4 navy blue squares 6½″ × 6½″.

3. Sew a purple 6½″ × 26″ strip to the black border on the top and bottom.

4. Sew a navy blue square to each end of the remaining 2 purple strips. Press seams toward the purple strips.

5. Sew an outer purple border with the navy blue squares to the black border on both sides.

6. Cut 5 strips 2½″ × width of fabric from remaining dark purple fabric for binding.

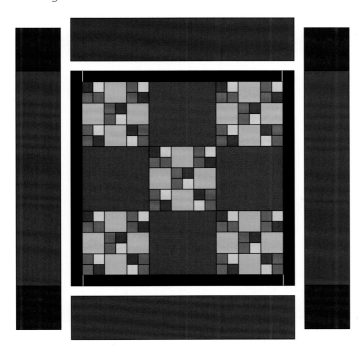

Quilt assembly

Quilting and Finishing

1. Mark quilting designs on the quilt top or plan to stitch without marking.

2. Layer and baste the quilt (see Layering and Basting in Quiltmaking Basics, page 123). Quilt by hand or machine.

3. Bind the quilt (see Binding in Quiltmaking Basics, page 123).

4. Make and attach a sleeve, if desired.

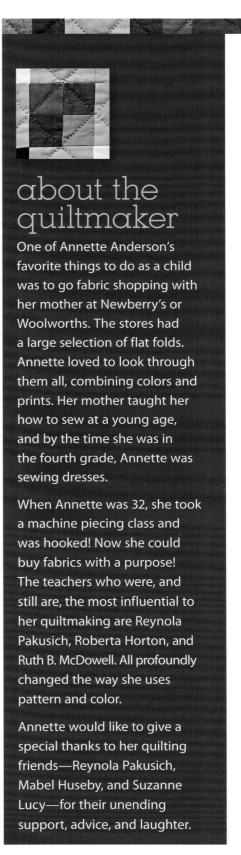

about the quiltmaker

One of Annette Anderson's favorite things to do as a child was to go fabric shopping with her mother at Newberry's or Woolworths. The stores had a large selection of flat folds. Annette loved to look through them all, combining colors and prints. Her mother taught her how to sew at a young age, and by the time she was in the fourth grade, Annette was sewing dresses.

When Annette was 32, she took a machine piecing class and was hooked! Now she could buy fabrics with a purpose! The teachers who were, and still are, the most influential to her quiltmaking are Reynola Pakusich, Roberta Horton, and Ruth B. McDowell. All profoundly changed the way she uses pattern and color.

Annette would like to give a special thanks to her quilting friends—Reynola Pakusich, Mabel Huseby, and Suzanne Lucy—for their unending support, advice, and laughter.

grandpa's quilt

FINISHED BLOCK: 12˝ × 12˝ | **FINISHED QUILT:** 68˝ × 84˝

Pieced by Carl Walters, quilted by Angela Walters

My grandpa made this quilt based on Amish quilts that he loved. He finished the top before he passed away four years ago. He was one of the most influential people in my life, as he was the one who taught me how to quilt and encouraged me to start machine quilting. Before he passed away, he made this quilt top as a gift for my daughter and gave it to me to machine quilt. I put it aside and didn't quilt it for a long time. But now that it is finished, it will be a cherished family heirloom that represents our final collaboration. This quilt, along with the stories of Grandpa and how he liked to quilt, will stay in our family for generations.

MATERIALS

Green solid fabric: 1¾ yards

Red solid fabric: 2⅓ yards

Blue solid fabric: 2¼ yards

Binding: ¾ yard

Backing: 5¼ yards

Batting: 74″ × 90″

CUTTING

Green solid fabric

Cut 4 strips 4½″ × width of fabric; subcut into 30 squares 4½″ × 4½″.

Cut 5 strips 2½″ × width of fabric; subcut into 80 squares 2½″ × 2½″.

Cut 4 strips 6⅞″ × width of fabric; subcut into 20 squares 6⅞″ × 6⅞″.

Red solid fabric

Cut 20 strips 2½″ × width of fabric; subcut into 80 rectangles 2½″ × 8½″.

Cut 4 strips 6⅞″ × width of fabric; subcut into 20 squares 6⅞″ × 6⅞″.

Blue solid fabric

Cut 17 strips 4½″ × width of fabric; subcut into 49 rectangles 4½″ × 12½″.

Binding fabric

Cut 9 strips 2½″ × width of fabric for double-fold binding.

construction

Assembly

1. Place a 6⅞″ × 6⅞″ red square on top of a 6⅞″ × 6⅞″ green square, right sides together. Sew ¼″ inside the edge all the way around the square.

2. Cut the square diagonally twice to create 4 half-square triangle units. Press seams open.

Cutting lines

Half-square triangle units

3. Sew the 4 half-square triangles together to make the center of the block. Repeat to make a total of 20 block centers. Press carefully. All of the edges are bias and will stretch easily.

Make 20.

4. Sew 1 red rectangle 2½″ × 8½″ to opposite sides of the center block.

5. Sew 1 small green square to each end of 2 other 2½″ × 8½″ red rectangles. Sew each of these 2 strips to the other sides of the center block. The block should now measure 12½″ × 12½″ square.

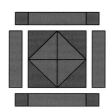

Block assembly

6. Sew a row of 4 pieced blocks alternating with 5 blue rectangles. Make 5.

7. Sew the horizontal sashing rows, alternating 4 blue rectangles and 5 green 4½″ × 4½″ squares. Make 6.

8. Lay out the rows, starting with a sashing row. Sew the rows together, matching seams between the block rows and the sashing rows.

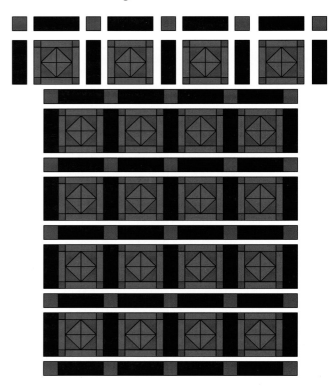

Quilt assembly

Quilting and Finishing

1. Mark quilting designs on the quilt top or plan to stitch without marking.

2. Layer and baste the quilt (see Layering and Basting in Quiltmaking Basics, page 123). Quilt by hand or machine.

3. Bind the quilt (see Binding in Quiltmaking Basics, page 123).

4. Make and attach a sleeve, if desired.

about the quiltmaker

Angela Walters is a machine quilter and author who loves to teach others to use quilting to bring out the best in their quilt tops. Her work has been published in numerous magazines and books, including two with C&T Publishing: *Free Motion Quilting with Angela Walters* and *In the Studio with Angela Walters*. She shares tips and finished quilts on her blog, www.quiltingismytherapy.com, and believes that "quilting is the funnest part!"

roman stripes

FINISHED BLOCK: $4\frac{1}{4}''$ × $4\frac{1}{4}''$ | **FINISHED QUILT:** $38\frac{1}{2}''$ × $38\frac{1}{2}''$

Made by Peggy Martin

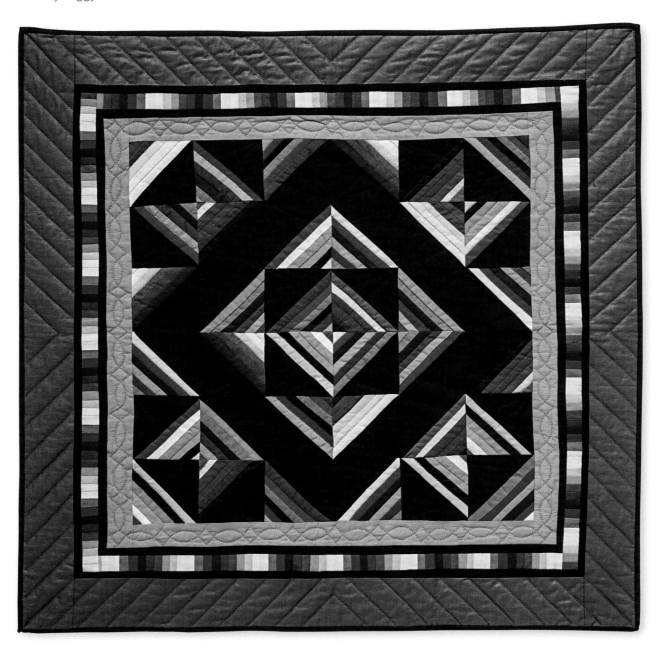

I had been quilting only two years when Roberta Horton's *An Amish Adventure* was published. I had always been interested in Amish quilts, so I jumped at the chance to take a workshop from Roberta when she came to my local guild a few years later. Her approach to the Amish colors and the concept of adding some "sparkle" to the quilt by using some clear light fabrics, along with the darker, more subdued ones, opened my eyes to working with color in new ways. She also had students separate their fabrics first by value and then by color. The concept of thinking this way about fabric was very exciting for me and helped me grow as a quilter. I began making some Roman Stripes blocks in that class.

Later that year, while visiting my in-laws in northeastern Ohio, my mother-in-law, Jennie Martin, took me on a tour of the Amish country in Holmes County. She was born and grew up there near Millersburg on a farm that had been sold to an Amish family by the time we visited. We drove down many unmarked dirt roads to several small towns that had dry goods stores and feed and tack stores that also sold fabric to Amish customers. I bought several yards of fabric, including some polished cotton solids, which I used in my Roman Stripes quilt.

I chose to set my Roman Stripes blocks in a modified barn-raising set, which I hand quilted.

MATERIALS

Amish-color solid fabrics: At least 9 or 10 fabrics in reds, pinks, blues, blue/greens, and purples to total 1½ yards for blocks and piano key border

Black solid fabric: 1⅜ yards for blocks, borders, and binding

Blue-green solid fabric: ⅜ yard for first border

Teal solid fabric: ½ yard for outer border

Backing fabric: 1½ yards of 45″-wide fabric

Batting: 45″ × 45″

CUTTING

All strips are cut from selvage to selvage and measure about 40˝ long. Fat quarters may be used for the Amish-color solids by cutting double the number of strips, about 20˝ long.

Amish-color solid fabrics

Cut 27 strips 1˝ × width of fabric for blocks.

Cut 9 or 10 strips 1˝ × width of fabric for piano key borders. Select a range from light to dark for shaded version of the border (page 94).

Black solid fabric

Cut 3 strips 5⅛˝ × width of fabric for blocks. (*Note:* This size may be adjusted to fit your blocks.)

Cut 4 strips 1˝ × width of fabric for second border.

Cut 4 strips 1˝ × width of fabric for fourth border.

Cut 5 strips 2½˝ × width of fabric for double-fold binding.

Blue-green solid fabric

Cut 4 strips 2˝ × width of fabric for first border.

Teal solid fabric

Cut 4 strips 3½˝ × width of fabric for outer border.

construction

Strip Set Assembly

1. Cut the 27 Amish-color solid 1˝-wide strips in half to make 54 strips about 20˝ long. This will make 9 strip sets.

2. Select 6 strips for the first strip set. Sew them together with a scant ¼˝ seam allowance. The strip set will be 3½˝ × 20˝.

3. Press all seams in the same direction.

Check for Accuracy

1. Make a copy of the Roman Stripes cutting guide (page 95).

2. Cut out the guide on the outer lines to make a paper template.

3. Place the paper template on the fabric strip set, with the long side of the triangle along the bottom edge of the strip set.

4. Make sure the strip set is exactly the height of the triangle.

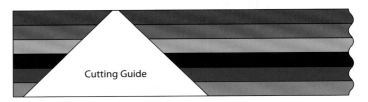

Check accuracy with cutting guide

NOTE

It is quite common to have the strip set be a little narrower, because the seam allowances take up some space. If the strip set is a little too small, either try sewing another set of strips with a slightly narrower seam allowance to get the accurate size or adjust the template to fit the narrower strip set. The template is exactly 3½˝ tall. If the strip set is 3¼˝, for example, adjust the template by trimming ¼˝ off the bottom (longest) edge of the cutting guide.

5. Make 8 more strip sets in the same manner, selecting different fabric combinations for each set. Be consistent—make sure that each strip set measures the same height as your first set.

How to Use the Cutting Guide

1. Place the cutting guide on the top corner of a right-angle acrylic triangle ruler, aligning the edges of the guide along the edges of the ruler.

2. Check to see whether the cutting guide's long bottom edge lies along one of the lines on the ruler.

3. Remove the cutting guide and use that line on the ruler as your guide for cutting triangles from the strip sets.

4. If the cutting guide does not align with a line on the triangle ruler, place a piece of masking tape on the ruler along the bottom edge of the cutting guide. (If a triangle ruler is unavailable, use a 6″ square-up ruler or a 5″ or larger rotary cutting ruler.) Place the paper cutting guide in one corner of the ruler, and place a piece of masking tape along the bottom edge of the cutting guide on the ruler. Remove the guide.

5. If you prefer to make a template for cutting, glue the cutting guide (as corrected, if necessary) to a piece of sturdy cardboard, and cut out accurately on the outer lines.

Create Triangles

1. To make the strip-set triangles, align the line on the acrylic ruler along the bottom edge of the strip set. *Note:* The tip of the acrylic ruler will hang over the strip set just slightly at the top.

2. Cut along both edges of the triangle to make the first fabric triangle.

3. Rotate the ruler so the guide line is along the top side of the strip set and the side of the new triangle lines up with the previously cut edge of strip.

4. Cut a triangle with its long edge at the top of the strip set.

Cut triangles from strip set.

5. Continue cutting triangles along the strip set, rotating the template each time. Triangles cut along the bottom will look different from triangles cut along the top, as the colors are in reverse order. This helps add to the scrappy look.

6. Each strip set will make 4 triangles. Cut all the strip sets to make a total of 36 triangles.

7. To make the black triangles, cut the 3 strips 5⅛″ × width of fabric into 18 squares 5⅛″ × 5⅛″. Subcut each diagonally once to make 36 triangles.

NOTE

If you have adjusted the size of your triangles, measure the short side of the adjusted triangle to get the size square for the black triangles.

Block Assembly

1. Sew each black triangle to a strip-set triangle to make 36 blocks. Press toward the black triangle.

Make 36 blocks.

2. Lay out the 36 blocks as shown in the quilt photo (page 90) and quilt assembly diagram (page 94).

3. Sew the blocks together in rows. Press seams in opposite directions from row to row.

Border Assembly

Refer to Butted Borders in Quiltmaking Basics (page 123).

Add First and Second Borders

1. Measure, cut, and sew the 2″ × width of fabric blue-green inner border strips to the quilt center.

2. Measure, cut, and sew the 1″ × width of fabric black second border strips to the quilt center.

Make Piano Key Border

This border may be shaded from light to dark (as in the quilt shown) or scrappy.

FOR SHADED VERSION:

1. Cut the 1″ × width of fabric strips in half to make the strip sets a manageable size.

2. Sew together the fabrics in order from light to dark to make 2 identical strip sets. Press toward the dark fabric.

3. Cut the strip sets into 1½″ strips.

4. Lay out the 1½″ strips in a continuing light-to-dark sequence (refer to the quilt photograph on page 90).

FOR SCRAPPY VERSION:

1. Cut the 1″ × width of fabric strips in half to make the strip sets a manageable size.

2. Sew the strips together to make 2 strip sets, arranging the fabrics in a different order in the second strip set for more variety. Press all seams in the same direction.

3. Cut the strip sets into 1½″ strips.

4. Lay out the 1½″ strips, alternating the sets, and turning them in different directions for a scrappy look.

Add Piano Key Border

1. Join the strips (either the shaded version or the scrappy version) to make 2 borders approximately 32″ long and 2 borders approximately 34″ long. These lengths allow for variations in the quilt size.

2. Measure the quilt and cut the 32″ long borders to fit the top and bottom of the quilt. Sew these borders to the quilt. Press seams toward the black border.

3. Measure the quilt and cut the 34″ long borders to fit the sides of the quilt. Sew these borders to the quilt. Press seams toward the black border.

Add Fourth Border and Outer Border

1. Measure, cut, and sew the 1″ × width of fabric black border strips to the quilt.

2. Measure, cut, and sew the 3½″ × width of fabric teal border strips to the quilt.

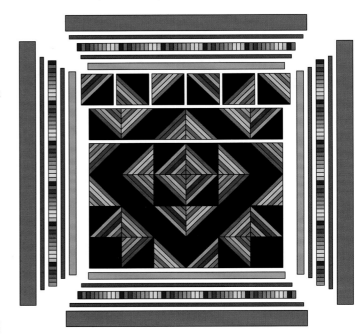

Quilt assembly

Quilting and Finishing

1. Mark quilting designs on the quilt top or plan to stitch without marking.

2. Layer and baste the quilt (see Layering and Basting in Quiltmaking Basics, page 123). Quilt by hand or machine.

3. Bind the quilt (see Binding in Quiltmaking Basics, page 123).

4. Make and attach a sleeve, if desired.

about the quiltmaker

Peggy Martin is an enthusiastic quilter and teacher specializing in fast and accurate quilting methods that offer many design possibilities. She specializes in color-play and building variations on traditional quilts. She began quilting in 1981 and became a teacher and lecturer in 1985. In 2010, she was chosen as Quilting Teacher of the Year by the International Association of Professional Quilters. She is the author of two books published by C&T: *Quick-Strip Paper Piecing* and *Paper Piece the Quick-Strip Way*, as well as a DVD. She also teaches her paper-piecing method in an online class at www.craftsy.com. Peggy is an award-winning quilter who has had quilts juried into many national shows. She lives in San Diego, California, and is married with two grown sons.

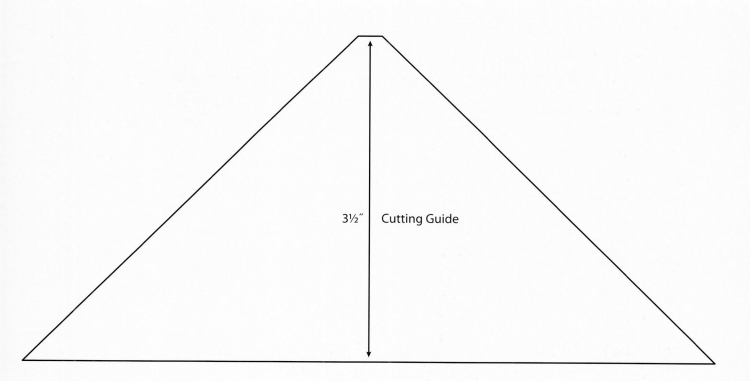

3½″ | Cutting Guide

Roman Stripes cutting guide

amirish butterflies

FINISHED BLOCK: 7½˝ × 7½˝ | **FINISHED QUILT:** 83˝ × 90½˝

Made by Linda Johansen

Why Amish?

I envy the Amish commitment to simplicity. I was raised to be a homemaker, and I love being one. I learned to sew on a treadle sewing machine and was raised without a television. A lack of outside distractions can make one focus on what is really needed to live—I keep trying to get there. When my boys were home, I made everything: bread, sauerkraut, sauces, curtains, rugs, quilts, and soap—everything I could. I still do much of that for the two of us, only now we also grow most of the food we eat during the summer. It sounds more complicated, but focusing on basics and daily needs actually simplifies life.

I love bright, intense colors, and what can show them off better than black? I enjoy the color and value movement in this quilt. The Amish use of color is not as simple as it might first seem. Their attention to value and use of complementary colors are often stunning as well as subtle.

I made *AmIrish Butterflies* about 25 years ago, and it is one of only three quilts that I have hand quilted. This quilt sat on a frame in our living room for two years; I would quilt an hour or so whenever I had a bit of time. The boys were still home then, so that wasn't often.

The name comes from the Irish Chain block pattern, the Amish colors, and the Japanese Sashiko butterfly quilting pattern.

MATERIALS

Solid-color fabrics: 8 colors, 8″ × 18″ each, for pieced blocks

Additional solid-color fabric: 1 yard for pieced blocks and inner border

Black fabric: 5½ yards* for blocks and outer border

Binding fabric: ¾ yard (It's best to get this fabric at the same time as your black background fabric if you want the blacks to match.)

Backing fabric: 7¾ yards

Batting: 89″ × 97″

* Requires 44″ usable fabric width.

CUTTING

Cut out the largest pieces from the black and inner border fabrics first: For the black fabric, cut the long outer border pieces, then cut the 8 strips. For the inner border fabric, cut the border pieces, then cut the 2″ strips.

Solid-color fabrics

Cut 9 strips 2″ × 8″ from each of the 8 colors for the blocks.

Additional solid-color fabric

Cut 7 strips 3″ × width of fabric for the inner border.

Cut 2 strips 2″ × width of fabric for the blocks. Subcut into 9 strips 2″ × 8″.

Black fabric

Cut 2 strips 9½″ × length of fabric for the outer border.

After cutting the long border strips, you will have a remainder of about 24″ × 5½ yards. Cut the remainder into 24 strips 8″ × 24″ for the blocks.

From 12 strips, cut 36 squares 8″ × 8″.

From 6 strips, cut 36 rectangles 3½″ × 8″.

From 6 strips, cut 72 rectangles 2″ × 8″.

Binding fabric

Cut 10 strips 2½″ × width of fabric for double-fold binding.

construction

Block Assembly

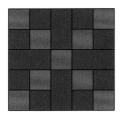

Completed block

These directions will make 4 blocks of 1 color at a time.

1. Sew a color strip 2″ × 8″ between 2 black strips 3½″ × 8″. Sew together along the 8″ side.

2. Cut the piece from Step 1 into 4 strips 2″ wide.

Cut 4 strips

3. Sew a color strip 2″ × 8″ to a black strip 2″ × 8″ along the 8″ side. Make 8.

4. Cut each of the pieces from Step 3 into 4 pieces 2″ wide. You will have 32 pieces 2″ × 3½″.

Cut 32 pieces.

5. Flip a piece from Step 4 vertically and sew it to another piece, right side up, to make a Four-Patch. Make 16.

Make 16 Four-Patch blocks.

6. Cut each of 2 black 3½″ × 8″ pieces into 4 pieces 2″ × 3½″ for a total of 8 pieces.

7. Lay out the block as shown. Sew the Four-Patch pieces to the black rectangles first. Make 2 rows. Then sew the rows to the strip with the color square in the center from Step 2.

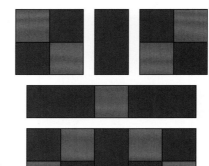

Block assembly—make 4 of each color.

8. Make 4 blocks in each of the remaining colors for a total of 36 blocks.

Quilt Assembly

1. Sew each of the pieced blocks to 1 black square 8″ × 8″. Sew the 2 pairs together to make a row of 4 pieced blocks alternating with 4 black squares. Make a total of 9 rows.

Make 9 rows.

2. Arrange the rows by color so that the first one starts with a solid black piece and the second one starts with a pieced block. The following rows will alternate. (Just flip the rows horizontally to change this orientation.)

3. Match the seams carefully and nest them together. Pin across the seams. Pin at an angle so that you can remove the pin right after you sew across the seam. Sew the rows together.

Borders

Refer to Butted Borders in Quiltmaking Basics (page 123).

1. Sew the 3″ × width of fabric inner border strips end-to-end to make a long strip. Measure, cut, and sew the inner borders to the quilt center.

2. Measure, cut, and sew the black 9½″ outer border to the quilt.

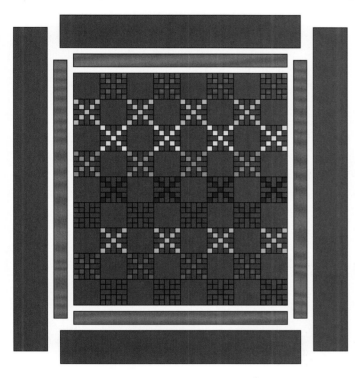

Quilt assembly

Quilting and Finishing

1. Mark quilting designs on the quilt top or plan to stitch without marking.

TIP

My quilting pattern for the finished 7½″ center block is modified from a traditional Japanese Sashiko pattern.

2. Layer and baste the quilt (see Layering and Basting in Quiltmaking Basics, page 123). Quilt by hand or machine.

3. Bind the quilt (see Binding in Quiltmaking Basics, page 123).

4. Make and attach a sleeve, if desired.

about the quiltmaker

Linda Johansen lives in western Oregon. She loves to quilt and to teach quilting—she especially enjoys getting others involved in something so satisfying, where there is something for everyone, no matter what they like. She also gardens, dances with her husband, and walks with her dogs. She has authored five Fast, Fun & Easy books and *Fabric Dyer's Dictionary* for C&T Publishing. Her fascination with the Amish goes back to her Quaker roots and a desire for simplicity in her life with fibromyalgia. Her interest in quilting began with hearing tales of her mother sitting under quilts at quilting bees and threading needles for the quilters. Visit her website at www.lindajohansen.com.

squared repeat

FINISHED QUILT: 60″ × 60″

Made by Terri Carpenter

The Amish quilt style has long been an inspiration for me. Their distinctive use of solid colors and their placement of blocks often evoke calmness and beauty with minimal effort. Using just solid fabric reduces the quilt pattern to its basic shape and helps emphasize the beauty inherent in these shapes. The solid fabrics also allow for more elaborate quilting by creating a backdrop for the stitches.

This style is no accident, yet it is not entirely due to artistic flare. It is a strong representation of the basic Amish tenets of humility, simplicity, and industriousness. Looking at their quilts, I'm easily reminded of how these tenets can be both useful and beautiful. I was inspired to do a quilt based on the traditional Square-within-a-Square block, which became the starting point for *Squared Repeat*. The use of only solid fabrics helps show off the basic shape and its subsequent expansion with each successive round.

This expansion is a more complex pattern that deviates from the simple Amish style, especially since the pattern is also set off-center. Amish quilts are generally symmetrical, often drawing your eye to the middle of the quilt. The colors in this quilt are also a little brighter than what's typically used by the Amish. Despite the opportunity to do more complex quilting on the solid fabrics, I kept it rather simple with straight lines. With its complex piecing and simpler quilting, *Squared Repeat* is in many ways the opposite of a traditional Lancaster County Amish quilt with its simpler piecing and more complex quilting.

MATERIALS

14 different solid fabrics are used to piece the top; refer to the table for each round.

ROUND	FABRIC COLOR	AMOUNT NEEDED
0	Brown	⅛ yard
1	Light green	⅛ yard
2	Light blue	⅛ yard
3	Medium blue	⅛ yard
4	Medium green	⅛ yard
5	Light green	⅛ yard
6	Dark blue	¼ yard
7	Medium blue	¼ yard
8	Medium green	⅓ yard
9	Red	½ yard
10	Light blue	⅝ yard
11	Medium blue	1½ yards
12	Dark green	1 yard
13	Medium green	1 yard

NOTE

This quilt is constructed by sewing each round of color onto the previous round to create the Square-within-a-Square. The first square is Round 0, and the last color added is Round 13. This project is organized by the order in which each round is sewn.

Binding fabric: ⅝ yard

Backing fabric: 4 yards

Batting: 66″ × 66″

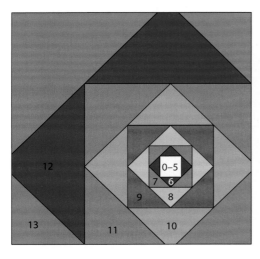

Schematic of rounds

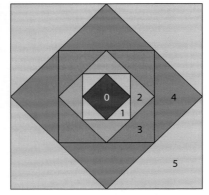

Detail schematic of Rounds 1–5

CUTTING

ROUND	FABRIC COLOR	CUTTING INSTRUCTION
0	Brown	Cut 1 square 1½″ × 1½″.
1	Light green	Cut 2 squares 1⅝″ × 1⅝″. Cut each on the diagonal once to create 4 triangles.
2	Light blue	Cut 2 squares 2″ × 2″. Cut each on the diagonal once to create 4 triangles.
3	Medium blue	Cut 2 squares 2⅜″ × 2⅜″. Cut each on the diagonal once to create 4 triangles.
4	Medium green	Cut 2 squares 3″ × 3″. Cut each on the diagonal once to create 4 triangles.
5	Light green	Cut 2 squares 3⅞″ × 3⅞″. Cut each on the diagonal once to create 4 triangles.
6	Dark blue	Cut 2 squares 5¼″ × 5¼″. Cut each on the diagonal once to create 4 triangles.
7	Medium blue	Cut 2 squares 7″ × 7″. Cut each on the diagonal once to create 4 triangles.
8	Medium green	Cut 2 squares 9½″ × 9½″. Cut each on the diagonal once to create 4 triangles.
9	Red	Cut 2 squares 13″ × 13″. Cut each on the diagonal once to create 4 triangles.
10	Light blue	Cut 2 squares 18″ × 18″. Cut each on the diagonal once to create 4 triangles (A).
11	Medium blue	Cut 1 square 25″ × 25″. Cut on the diagonal once to create 2 triangles (B).
		Cut 1 square 22″ × 22″. Cut on the diagonal once to create 2 triangles (C).
12	Dark green	Cut 1 square 32⅞″ × 32⅞″. Cut on the diagonal once to create 2 triangles (E).
13	Medium green	Cut 1 square 32″ × 32″. Cut on the diagonal once to create 2 triangles (F).

construction

Press all seams away from center.

Assembly

Round 0

Mark the center of each side of the brown fabric square.

Round 1

1. Mark the center of the long side of each light green triangle.

2. Sew 2 light green triangles to opposite sides of the brown square, lining up the center marks. Press.

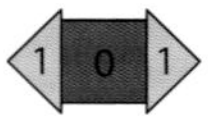

Round 0 and start of Round 1

3. Sew the remaining 2 light green triangles to the brown square, again matching the center marks.

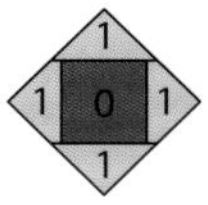

Finished Round 1 square

Round 2

1. Center and sew 2 light blue triangles to opposite sides of the previous round of light green. Press.

2. Center and sew the remaining 2 light blue triangles to the light green square. Press.

Finished Round 2 square

Rounds 3–9

Repeat the steps in Round 2 for each round of triangles to form a larger square with each successive round. Complete through Round 9 with the addition of the red triangles.

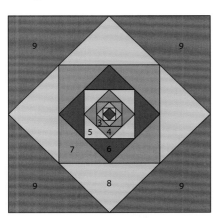

Finished Round 9 square

Round 10

1. For 2 triangles A: Measure and mark a line 9½″ from the base of the triangle. Baste below the marked line to stabilize the fabric. Cut away the tip of triangle on the marked line, leaving the basted stitches on the triangle base.

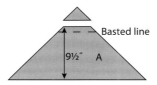

Triangle A basted with top cut away—Make 2.

2. Center and sew 1 full triangle and 1 triangle base A on opposite sides of the previous round of red fabric. Press. Sew the remaining full triangle and triangle base A to the red square. Press.

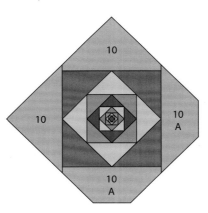

Finished Round 10

NOTE

The quilt top is now directional. The 2 cut triangles from Round 10 make up part of the quilt edge on the bottom and right side.

Round 11

1. From 1 triangle B: Measure and mark 19″ from the top corner on each of the sides. Line up the marks with a ruler and cut to make a new triangle D.

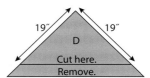

Triangle B cut to form new triangle D

2. Orient the quilt as shown in the finished Round 10 diagram (at left). Sew the 2 medium triangles C to the upper right side and lower left side of the square. Press. Sew the remaining triangle B to the upper left of the square. Sew triangle D to the lower right of the square. Press.

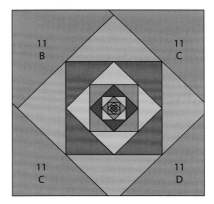

Finished Round 11 square

Round 12

1. For the 2 triangles E: Measure and mark a line 15½″ from the base of the triangle. Baste below the marked line to stabilize the fabric. Cut away the tip of the triangle on the marked line, leaving the basted stitches on the triangle base.

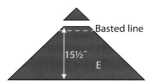

Triangle E basted with top cut away—Make 2.

2. Center and sew the triangle bases E to the top and left sides of the quilt. Press after each addition.

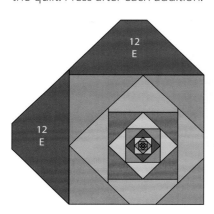

Finished Round 12

Round 13

1. From 1 triangle F: Measure and mark 16″ from the bottom corner on each of the sides. Line up the ruler on the side at the mark and cut to form 2 smaller triangles G.

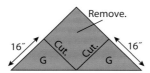

Triangle F cut to form 2 new triangles G

2. Sew the remaining triangle F to the upper left corner of the quilt. Press. Sew triangles G to the upper right and lower left corners of the quilt. Press.

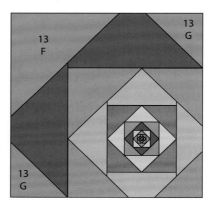

Finished Round 13

Quilting and Finishing

1. Mark quilting designs on the quilt top or plan to stitch without marking.

2. Layer and baste the quilt (see Layering and Basting in Quiltmaking Basics, page 123). Quilt by hand or machine.

3. Bind the quilt (see Binding in Quiltmaking Basics, page 123).

4. Make and attach a sleeve, if desired.

about the quiltmaker

Terri Carpenter first became aware of quilting by sleeping under the functional patchwork quilts her grandmother made. She has no memories of watching her grandmother sew, but she cherishes the memories of her and her quilts. The second time she became aware of quilting was in her teenage years, while visiting a family friend. The friend was in the midst of basting a very large and artistic quilt top. It was then that Terri made the connection between her grandmother's functional quilts and the artistic beauty of her friend's quilt, and she became enthralled with quilting. She finished her first quilt not long after that visit in 1994. She currently belongs to the East Bay Modern Quilt Guild and shares her love of quilting through her blog, www.thequiltedfox.blogspot.com.

it's hip to be square

FINISHED BLOCK: 9″ × 9″ | **FINISHED QUILT:** 63″ × 81″

Made by Michelle Webber

Every aspect of Amish quilting is inspiring. The lines and shapes of the patterns are basic yet bold. The simplicity creates a timeless modernism that is as intriguing today as it was at the turn of the last century. The bright colors are whimsical and joyful and seem to be effortlessly combined. The assortment of colors can be as simple as two colors or a totally scrappy look. With the wide-open spaces of piecing and borders, mixed with the smooth texture of the solid-colored fabrics, comes the opportunity for the third dimension of the project—the fine quilting. The patterns are sometimes simple and sometimes complex, but always beautiful.

This modern interpretation of the Amish style borrows classic characteristics but adds a twist. The solid-style fabrics are classic, as is the black, wide border. The original Amish communities had their unique palettes that defined their settlements. This modern quilt holds true to tradition in the block centers and frames but breaks with tradition in the rings. These rings are modern colors selected for their brightness and variety, without regard to community rules. I used whatever combinations looked appealing, creating almost a collection of mini quilts. As with the original Amish quilts, the piecing is simple, and the color impact is bold. The quilting shown on this quilt is simple; however, with its wide border, other choices could be used. Amish designs fit with many home styles.

MATERIALS

Medium-to-dark solid fabrics in muted tones: At least 12 different fabrics, ¼–⅜ yard each, for block centers and outer frames (Even subtle variety within color families will add interest and aid in arranging.)

Clear bright-colored fabrics: A large variety in small amounts, approximately ⅛ yard or less each, for the rings (Colors may be repeated, but repeats must be placed in different ring positions.)

Solid black fabric: 1⅞ yards for border and ⅝ yard for binding

Batting: 69″ × 87″

Backing fabric: 5 yards

CUTTING

Medium-to-dark solid fabrics in muted tones

Cut strips 2¾″ × width of fabric for the outer frames and center squares.

For 1 block:

Cut 2 rectangles 2¾″ × 5″.

Cut 2 rectangles 2¾″ × 9½″.

Cut 1 square 2¾″ × 2¾″.

Repeat to create 35 sets.

Clear bright-colored fabrics

Cut strips ⅞″ × width of fabric for the 3 rings.

For 1 block:

Cut 2 rectangles ⅞″ × 2¾″ for inner ring.

Cut 2 rectangles ⅞″ × 3½″ for inner ring.

Cut 2 rectangles ⅞″ × 3½″ for center ring.

Cut 2 rectangles ⅞″ × 4¼″ for center ring.

Cut 2 rectangles ⅞″ × 4¼″ for outer ring.

Cut 2 rectangles ⅞″ × 5″ for outer ring.

Repeat to create 35 sets.

Border fabric

Cut 4 lengthwise strips 9½″ × length of fabric.

Binding fabric

Cut 8 strips 2½″ × width of the fabric for double-fold binding.

Backing

Cut fabric in half crosswise.

construction

Block Assembly

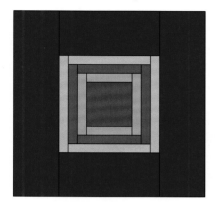

Completed block

1. Arrange each block as a mini quilt, creating a pleasing combination of colors.

2. Sew 2 short inner ring rectangles to opposite sides of the 2¾″ × 2¾″ center square. Press seams away from the center square.

3. Sew 2 remaining inner ring rectangles to the other 2 sides of the center square. Press seams away from the center square.

4. Repeat this sequence using the center ring strips, the outer ring strips, and the outer frame strips. The block will measure 9½″ × 9½″. Make 35.

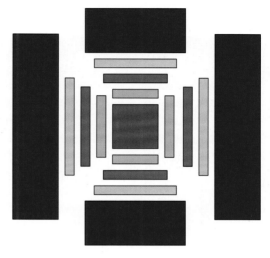

Block assembly

Quilt Assembly

1. Arrange the blocks on your design wall or a large flat surface in 5 rows of 7 blocks each.

2. Sew the blocks together into rows. Press the seam allowances in one direction for odd-numbered rows and in the opposite direction for even-numbered rows.

3. Sew the rows together. Press seams in one direction.

4. Measure, cut, and sew a border strip to the top and bottom of the quilt. Press seams toward the border strips. Repeat this step for the side border strips. (Refer to Butted Borders in Quiltmaking Basics, page 123.)

5. For the backing, trim selvages and join the 2 pieces lengthwise. Trim off the excess width from one side to make the backing 69″ wide.

Quilting and Finishing

1. Mark quilting designs on the quilt top or plan to stitch without marking.

2. Layer and baste the quilt (see Layering and Basting in Quiltmaking Basics, page 123). Quilt by hand or machine.

3. Bind the quilt (see Binding in Quiltmaking Basics, page 123).

4. Make and attach a sleeve, if desired.

about the quiltmaker

Michelle Webber is a southern California native. At an early age, she showed a deep interest in fabrics and textile arts. She received her first real sewing machine at the age of ten and had made more than 30 quilts before taking her first quilting class! As an adult, she moved to northern California, where she joined a guild and discovered a whole new dimension to quilting. Michelle is interested in a variety of quilt styles, with color being of special interest to her.

amish squares

FINISHED BLOCK: 6″ × 6″ | **FINISHED QUILT:** 66″ × 66″

Designed and made by Monique Dillard; quilted by Sue Glorch

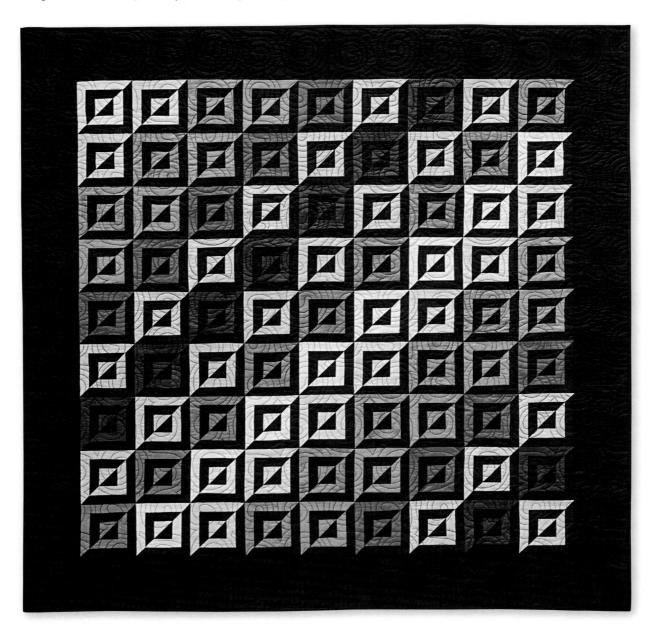

One of the things that draws me to Amish quilts is the black background, which gives the quilts a very dramatic look. I wanted to use a graduation of color from light to medium to dark for a colorwash effect. In this quilt, the alternating use of color and black within each block provides a dramatic sense of depth. It also shows how effective fade out (page 10) can be.

Fabric: Memories of Provence by Monique Dillard for Maywood Studio

MATERIALS

Solid-color fabrics: 9 different colors, ½ yard each

Black solid fabric: 4¼ yards for blocks, borders, and binding

Backing fabric: 4¼ yards

Batting: 72″ × 72″

CUTTING

Solid-color fabrics

Cut 1 strip 4⅛″ × width of fabric. Subcut into 3 squares 4⅛″ × 4⅛″. Cut each square diagonally twice. From the remainder, cut 2 strips 1½″ × approximately 27″. Subcut 9 pieces 1½″ × 4⅞″.

Cut 5 strips 1½″ × width of fabric. Subcut into 9 pieces 1½″ × 3⅞″, 9 pieces 1½″ × 5⅞″, and 9 pieces 1½″ × 6⅞″.

Black solid fabric

Cut 3 strips 4⅛″ × width of fabric. Subcut into 21 squares 4⅛″ × 4⅛″. Cut each square diagonally twice.

Cut 46 strips 1½″ × width of fabric. Subcut into 81 pieces 1½″ × 6⅞″, 81 pieces 1½″ × 5⅞″, 81 pieces 1½″ × 4⅞″, and 81 pieces 1½″ × 3⅞″.

Cut 7 strips 6½″ × width of fabric for border.

Cut 8 strips 2½″ × width of fabric for double-fold binding.

construction

Block Assembly

1. Sew 1 black piece 1½″ × 3⅞″ to the side of a solid color triangle cut from a 4⅛″ × 4⅛″ square. Press toward the black. Repeat to make 9.

Make 9.

2. Sew 1 black piece 1½″ × 4⅞″ to the top of the triangle from Step 1. Press toward the black. Repeat to make 9.

Make 9.

3. Using the same solid color as in Step 1, sew a solid color piece 1½″ × 5⅞″ to the side of the piece from Step 2. Press toward the black. Repeat to make 9.

Make 9.

4. Using the same solid color as in Step 1, sew a solid-color piece 1½″ × 6⅞″ to the top of the piece from Step 3. Press toward the black. Repeat to make 9.

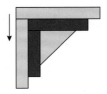

Make 9.

5. With a rotary cutter and ruler, trim the piece from Step 4 even with the long side of the center triangle. Repeat for all 9 pieces.

Make 9.

6. Using the same solid color used in the above steps, sew 1 solid piece 1½″ × 3⅞″ to the side of a black triangle cut from a 4⅛″ × 4⅛″ square. Press toward the black. Repeat to make 9.

Make 9.

7. Sew 1 piece 1½″ × 4⅞″ of the same solid color to the top of the triangle from Step 6. Press toward the black. Repeat to make 9.

Make 9.

8. Sew 1 black piece 1½″ × 5⅞″ to the side of the piece from Step 7. Press toward the black. Repeat to make 9.

Make 9.

9. Sew 1 black piece 1½″ × 6⅞″ to the top of the piece from Step 8. Press toward the black. Repeat to make 9.

Make 9.

10. With a rotary cutter and ruler, trim the piece from Step 9 even with the long side of the center triangle. Repeat for all 9 pieces.

Make 9.

11. Using the pieces from Steps 5 and 10, sew the block halves together to make a block. Press the seams in one direction. The block should measure 6½″ × 6½″, including seam allowance.

12. Repeat Steps 1–11 to make 9 blocks from each of the remaining 8 colors. There will be a total of 81 blocks.

Make 9 in each color.

Quilt Assembly

Refer to the quilt photo (page 109) and the quilt assembly diagram. Follow the arrows for pressing directions.

1. Arrange your quilt in horizontal rows, making sure that the solid colors are arranged in diagonal rows. Sew together, pressing seams in alternate direction from row to row.

2. Sew the 7 black 6½″ × width of fabric border strips together end-to-end. Press. Cut 2 strips 6½″ × 65″ for the side borders. Cut 2 strips 6½″ × 72″ for the top and bottom borders. Note that the borders are cut long for ease of mitering.

3. Sew the side borders to the quilt, then add the top and bottom borders. Complete the mitered corners using your favorite method,

or see the instructions in C&T's Quiltmaking Basics at www.ctpub.com > Resources > Consumer Resources: Quiltmaking Basics.

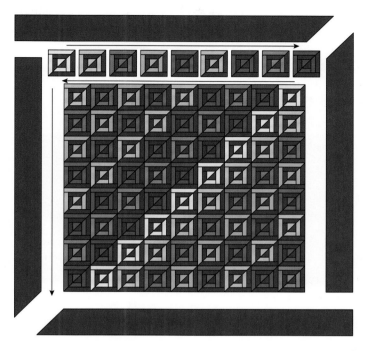

Quilt assembly

Quilting and Finishing

1. Mark quilting designs on the quilt top or plan to stitch without marking.

2. Layer and baste the quilt (see Layering and Basting in Quiltmaking Basics, page 123). Quilt by hand or machine.

3. Bind the quilt (see Binding in Quiltmaking Basics, page 123).

4. Make and attach a sleeve, if desired.

about the quiltmaker

Monique Dillard of Rockford, Illinois, was born in Winnipeg, Manitoba, Canada where she learned handwork and sewing. She parlayed her degree in mathematics into a genuine understanding of the need for accurate ¼″ seams, squared blocks, and precise cutting. After teaching regularly at her local quilt shop for 15 years, she now teaches nationally and runs her online quilting business www.opengatequilts.com. Monique's classes and retreats always fill up fast with fans from previous classes and students eager to learn from this talented designer.

fall colors

FINISHED BLOCK: 4˝ × 4˝ | **FINISHED QUILT:** 82˝ × 98˝ (includes 2˝-wide binding)

Made by Veronica Haberthuer

For this quilt, I was inspired by the leaves of trees in the fall, with the bright blue of the sky peeking through. When we drove through the country roads of New England, we would take many pictures of the beautifully colored trees. The quilting in the border represents the road we traveled, with squares representing the pictures taken along the way.

MATERIALS

Dark gray fabric*: 1⅞ yards for outer border

Rust fabric*: 1⅞ yards for blocks and outer border

Lime green fabric: 3 yards for blocks and 2″-wide binding

Black fabric: 8 yards for narrow inner border and backing

Fall-colored fabrics: approximately ⅜ yard of each of about 11 different fall colors in green, orange, and yellow

Bright sky-blue fabric: ⅜ yard

Batting: 88″ × 104″

* Requires 42″ usable fabric width.

CUTTING

Lime green fabric

Cut 10 strips 8¾″ × width of fabric for 2″-wide double-fold binding. Put leftover fabric with the fall-colored fabrics.

Rust fabric

Cut these strips lengthwise on fabric.

Cut 1 strip 10½″ × 33½″ (A).

Cut 1 strip 10½″ × 24½″ (B).

Cut 1 strip 10½″ × 46½″ (C).

Cut 1 strip 10½″ × 26½″ (D).

Put leftover fabric with the fall-colored fabrics.

Dark gray fabric

Cut these strips lengthwise on fabric:

Cut 1 strip 10½″ × 51½″ (A).

Cut 1 strip 10½″ × 44½″ (B).

Cut 1 strip 10½″ × 38½″ (C).

Cut 1 strip 10½″ × 42½″ (D).

Black fabric

Cut 7 strips 1½″ × width of fabric.

Use the remaining black yardage for quilt backing.

Fall-colored fabrics

Cut 242 squares 4½″ × 4½″.

Cut strips from the scrap fabric, ranging from 1¼″ to 2¼″ wide and at least 4½″ long, for embellishing the squares.

Bright sky-blue fabric

Cut at least 10 squares 4½″ × 4½″.

construction

TIPS

- Pin carefully and ease fabrics as needed.
- Press all seams to one side as you sew.

Embellished Block Assembly

Approximately 56 blocks are embellished with varying widths of contrasting colors.

1. Using the fall-colored fabrics, select a strip to sew onto a 4½″ × 4½″ square. Cut a 4½″ length from this strip.

2. Place the strip face down on the square. Sew it to the square using a ¼″ seam.

3. Cut the square at the edge of the strip.

Cut.

4. Sew the cut-off piece of the square to the remaining edge of the strip. Press. Trim the block to 4½″ × 4½″.

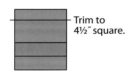
Trim to 4½″ square.

5. Repeat Steps 1–4 to create a total of 56 blocks.

Quilt Assembly

1. Arrange the embellished blocks, the sky blue squares, and the remaining fall-colored squares on your design wall or a large flat surface to make a pleasing arrangement.

2. Sew pieces together in rows of 14 pieces each. Make 18 rows. Press seams in alternating directions from row to row.

3. Sew rows together. Press.

Borders

1. Sew the 7 black 1½″ inner border strips end-to-end. Cut 2 strips 1½″ × 72½″ and 2 strips 1½″ × 58½″.

2. Pin and sew the 1½″ × 72½″ black borders to the sides of the quilt.

3. Pin and sew the 1½″ × 58½″ black borders to the top and bottom of the quilt.

4. Sew the 10½″ outer border strips together, matching A, B, C, and D pieces cut from the rust and dark gray fabrics. Press seams toward the dark fabric.

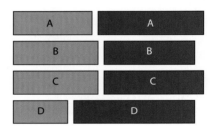

Outer border strips

5. Pin and sew strip A to the right side of the quilt, leaving the seam open about 12˝ at the bottom (see quilt assembly diagram, page 116). Press.

6. Pin and sew strip B to the top of the quilt, strip C to the left side, and strip D to the quilt bottom. Press after completing each seam.

7. Sew the rest of strip A to the right side of the quilt. Press.

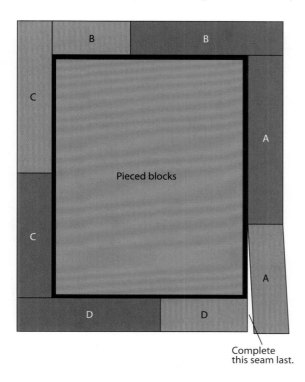

Complete this seam last.

Quilt assembly

Quilting and Finishing

1. Mark quilting designs on the quilt top or plan to stitch without marking.

2. For backing, cut 3 black pieces 88˝ × width of fabric. Sew together along the 88˝ sides.

3. Layer and baste the quilt (see Layering and Basting in Quiltmaking Basics, page 123). Quilt by hand or machine.

4. When squaring up this quilt, leave 1¾˝ of batting and backing beyond the edges of the quilt top on all sides. This extra along with the ¼˝ binding seam allowance will fill the 2˝-wide binding. Join the 8¾˝ × width of fabric strips end-to-end with straight, not diagonal, seams.

5. Bind the quilt (see Binding in Quiltmaking Basics, page 123).

6. Make and attach a sleeve, if desired.

about the quiltmaker

Veronica Haberthuer has been quilting since 1976. Her quilts have won the Juror's Choice Award in Alaska's Earth, Fire, and Fibre show and have been juried into Quilt San Diego's Visions: QuiltArt.

just around the corner

FINISHED QUILT: 32″ × 32″

Made by Karen Hansen Tyler

I was having an especially difficult time during 1984. A lot of situations had developed in my life that made for many dark moments. I felt that I was "boxed in," and just when I thought I had broken free … well, I was "boxed in" yet again.

It isn't unusual for me to dream in color or for my dreams to then take shape in the form of a quilt. What was unusual was to dream in Amish colors and to have a passion to incorporate a style of quilting that was very foreign to me. I knew that I needed to take this journey to find the "Amish" in my life.

There are 1,148 pieces in this quilt top, and I made it in less than six weeks while in a car traveling to Milwaukee. As I pieced away the miles, I thought about the book that Roberta Horton had written two years earlier about Amish quilting. I found myself comforted by thoughts of all the Amish women who used black cloth and bits of bright to make sense of their place in this world and the next. When I had finished the last stitch, I knew that the pain I had been carrying around had been put to rest.

I feel that my quilt expresses the Bible verse that talks about no matter how dark and sad a time may be in your life, there will always be light (God).

As you look at my wallhanging, imagine the dark black boxes as a tunnel and the bits of light around the boxes leading you to the light found right in the center. There, I hope you find what I did—the knowledge that hope and peace are just around the corner.

MATERIALS

Black fabric: 2⅞ yards for piecing, backing, and binding

Maroon fabric: ¼ yard

Rust fabric: ¼ yard

Brown fabric: ¼ yard

Dark purple fabric: ¼ yard

Purple-pink fabric: ¼ yard

Light purple fabric: ¼ yard

Dark red fabric: ⅛ yard

Medium red fabric: ¼ yard

Bright red fabric: ⅛ yard

Low-loft batting or flannel: 38˝ × 38˝

CUTTING—FABRICS

All strips are cut the width of the fabric.

Black fabric

Cut 24 strips 1½″ wide. Subcut into 620 squares 1½″ × 1½″.

Cut 4 strips 2″ wide. Subcut into 62 squares 2″ × 2″. Cut each in half diagonally once to make 124 triangles.

Cut 4 strips 2½″ × width of fabric for double-fold binding.

Cut 1 square 38″ × 38″ for the backing.

Maroon fabric

Cut 2 strips 1½″ wide. Subcut into 48 squares 1½″ × 1½″.

Cut 1 strip 2″ wide. Subcut into 4 squares 2″ × 2″. Cut each in half diagonally once to make 8 triangles.

Rust fabric

Cut 2 strips 1½″ wide. Subcut into 32 squares 1½″ × 1½″.

Cut 1 strip 2″ wide. Subcut into 8 squares 2″ × 2″. Cut each in half diagonally once to make 16 triangles.

Brown fabric

Cut 2 strips 1½″ wide. Subcut into 32 squares 1½″ × 1½″.

Cut 1 strip 2″ wide. Subcut into 8 squares 2″ × 2″. Cut each in half diagonally once to make 16 triangles.

Dark purple fabric

Cut 2 strips 1½″ wide. Subcut into 40 squares 1½″ × 1½″.

Cut 1 strip 2″ wide. Subcut into 18 squares 2″ × 2″. Cut each in half diagonally once to make 36 triangles.

Purple-pink fabric

Cut 3 strips 1½″ wide. Subcut into 64 squares 1½″ × 1½″.

Cut 1 strip 2″ wide. Subcut into 4 squares 2″ × 2″. Cut each in half diagonally once to make 8 triangles.

Light purple fabric

Cut 2 strips 1½″ wide. Subcut into 40 squares 1½″ × 1½″.

Cut 1 strip 2″ wide. Subcut into 12 squares 2″ × 2″. Cut each in half diagonally once to make 24 triangles.

Dark red fabric

Cut 1 strip 2″ wide. Subcut into 4 squares 2″ × 2″. Cut each in half diagonally once to make 8 triangles.

Medium red fabric

Cut 1 strip 1½″ wide. Subcut into 8 squares 1½″ × 1½″.

Cut 1 strip 2″ wide. Subcut into 4 squares 2″ × 2″. Cut each in half diagonally once to make 8 triangles.

Bright red fabric

Cut 1 strip 1½″ wide. Subcut into 16 squares 1½″ × 1½″.

CUTTING—PAPER

You may choose to cut your own paper pieces from a heavy-weight paper. I like to use index cards or old file folders. This is time-consuming, however, so you may wish to purchase some of the many ready-made pieces available from your local quilt store. Remember not to throw out used paper pieces—you can use them in a future project!

Cut 900 squares 1″ × 1″.

Cut 124 squares 1″ × 1″. Cut each diagonally once to make 248 triangles.

construction

Prepare the Fabric Paper-Pieced Units

Pin the paper squares and triangles to the wrong side of the corresponding cut fabric shapes. The extra fabric around each paper piece should be approximately ¼˝ wide. Trim if desired; your seam allowance doesn't have to be exact in this process.

- **Black:** 620 squares and 124 triangles
- **Maroon:** 48 squares and 8 triangles
- **Rust:** 32 squares and 16 triangles
- **Brown:** 32 squares and 16 triangles
- **Dark purple:** 40 squares and 36 triangles
- **Purple-pink:** 64 squares and 8 triangles
- **Light purple:** 40 squares and 24 triangles
- **Dark red:** 8 triangles
- **Medium red:** 8 squares and 8 triangles
- **Bright red:** 16 squares

Baste the Paper-Pieced Units

Make the 1˝ × 1˝ Units

Fold the fabric around the paper shape. Using a sewing needle and light thread (you may use water-soluble glue instead), baste the fabric to the paper through all 3 layers. Wrap and stitch around the entire square shape. Leave about a 1˝ tail and don't knot the end of your thread.

Make the Triangle Units

Fold the fabric around the paper shape, taking special care with the sharp points. Baste around the entire triangle shape through all 3 layers. Leave about 1˝ tail and don't knot the end of your thread.

Sew

Sew the Triangle Units

Place 2 triangle units right sides together. Using a needle and thread, whipstitch the units together to form the number indicated below:

1 black triangle + 1 dark purple triangle = 1˝ × 1˝ square. Make 36 squares.

Make 36.

1 black triangle + 1 maroon triangle = 1˝ × 1˝ square. Make 8 squares.

Make 8.

1 black triangle + 1 rust triangle = 1˝ × 1˝ square. Make 16 squares.

Make 16.

1 black triangle + 1 purple-pink triangle = 1˝ × 1˝ square. Make 8 squares.

Make 8.

1 black triangle + 1 dark red triangle = 1″ × 1″ square. Make 8 squares.

Make 8.

1 black triangle + 1 medium red triangle = 1″ × 1″ square. Make 8 squares.

Make 8.

1 black triangle + 1 light purple triangle = 1″ × 1″ square. Make 24 squares.

Make 24.

1 black triangle + 1 brown triangle = 1″ × 1″ square. Make 16 squares.

Make 16.

Quilt Assembly

1. Arrange the basted paper pieces (squares) on a flat surface according to the quilt layout.

Quilt layout

2. Starting with the first row and working left to right, join each unit by placing right sides together and whipstitching. Repeat this step with each row.

3. Starting with the first completed row and working top to bottom, join each row by placing right sides together and whipstitching. Make sure the seams intersect correctly. Repeat this step until the quilt top is completed.

4. From the right side of the quilt top, carefully remove the basting stitches.

5. Turn over the quilt top and, from the back side, pop out the paper pieces.

6. Lightly press from the back side of the quilt, if needed.

Quilting and Finishing

1. Mark quilting designs on the quilt top or plan to stitch without marking. Hand or machine quilt in-the-ditch between each square, if desired.

2. Layer and baste the quilt (see Layering and Basting in Quiltmaking Basics, page 123). Quilt by hand or machine.

3. Bind the quilt. (For measuring and cutting instructions, see Binding in Quiltmaking Basics, page 123.) Instead of attaching the binding with a ¼″ seam, turn under the binding seam allowance and whipstitch to the front of the quilt. Fold binding to the back and blindstitch.

4. Make and attach a sleeve, if desired.

about the quiltmaker

In 1978, Karen Hansen Tyler was watching her children grow up and taking a beginning quilting class from Roberta Horton. Roberta was just starting out on her famous path, and Karen was falling in love with turning scraps of fabric into works of art.

Karen's quilting has moved from using traditional patterns and techniques to her current original quilt designs. With more than 30 years of experimenting and manipulating fabric, she has learned that the next new project is always just around the corner.

Today, Karen continues to use her quilts as a form of journaling. She tries to share her love of quilting with everyone she meets. She lives in Indianapolis with her husband, Ross, and dog, Toby. When she is not at home, you will find her playing with her grown children and grandchildren.

quiltmaking basics:
how to finish your quilt

general guidelines

Seam Allowances

A ¼″ seam allowance is used unless otherwise specified. It's a good idea to do a test seam before you begin sewing to check that your ¼″ is accurate. Accuracy is the key to successful piecing.

There is no need to backstitch. Seamlines will be crossed by another seam, which will anchor them.

Pressing

In general, press seams toward the darker fabric. Press lightly in an up-and-down motion. Avoid using a very hot iron or overironing, which can distort shapes and blocks. Be especially careful when pressing bias edges, as they stretch easily.

borders

When border strips are cut on the crosswise grain, piece the strips together to achieve the needed lengths.

Butted Borders

In most cases, the side borders are sewn on first.

When you have finished the quilt top, measure it through the center vertically. This will be the length to cut the side borders. Place pins at the centers of all four sides of the quilt top, as well as in the center of each side border strip. Pin the side borders to the quilt top first, matching the center pins. Using a ¼″ seam allowance, sew the borders to the quilt top and press toward border.

Measure horizontally across the center of the quilt top, including the side borders. This will be the length to cut the top and bottom borders. Repeat pinning, sewing, and pressing as you did for the side borders.

backing

Plan on making the backing a minimum of 6″ longer and wider than the quilt top. Piece the backing, if necessary. Trim the selvages before you piece to the desired size. To economize, piece the back from any leftover quilting fabrics or blocks in your collection.

batting

The type of batting to use is a personal decision; consult your local quilt shop. Cut batting approximately 6″ longer and wider than your quilt top. Note that your batting choice will affect how much quilting is necessary for the quilt. Check the manufacturer's instructions to see how far apart the quilting lines can be.

layering

Spread the backing wrong side up and tape down the edges with masking tape. (If you are working on carpet, you can use T-pins to secure the backing to the carpet.) Center the batting on top, smoothing out any folds. Place the quilt top right side up on top of the batting and backing, making sure it is centered.

basting

Basting keeps the quilt "sandwich" layers from shifting while you quilt.

If you plan to machine quilt, pin baste the quilt layers together with safety pins placed about 3″–4″ apart. Begin basting in the center and move toward the edges, first in vertical and then horizontal rows. Try not to pin directly on the intended quilting lines.

If you plan to hand quilt, baste the layers together with thread, using a long needle and light-colored thread. Knot one end of the thread. Using stitches approximately the length of the needle, begin in the center and move out toward the edges in vertical and horizontal rows that are approximately 4″ apart. Then stitch two diagonal rows of basting.

quilting

Quilting, whether by hand or machine, enhances the quilt's design. You may choose to quilt in-the-ditch, echo the piecing, use patterns from quilting design books and stencils, or do your own free-motion quilting. Remember to check your batting manufacturer's recommendations for how close the quilting lines must be.

binding

Trim excess batting and backing from the quilt so it is even with the edges of the quilt top.

Amish quilts are traditionally finished with butted binding (page 125). Instructions for binding with mitered corners are also included (page 126).

Binding Strips

1. For ¼″ finished double-fold binding, cut the binding strips 2½″ wide and piece them together with diagonal seams to make strips the required length.

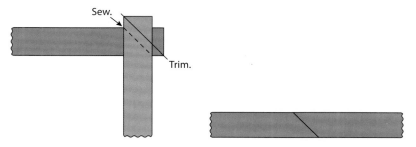

Sew from corner to corner. Completed diagonal seam

2. Trim the seam allowance to ¼″. Press the seams open.

3. Press the entire strip in half lengthwise, wrong sides together.

Double-Fold Butted Binding

1. Measure the quilt through the center from side to side. Piece or trim 2 binding strips to that measurement plus 1″. On the top edge of the quilt, line up the raw edges of the binding with the raw edge of the quilt. Let the binding extend ½″ past the corners of the quilt. Sew with a ¼″ seam allowance. Repeat this step for the bottom edge of the quilt.

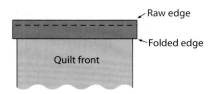

Attach binding to front of quilt.

2. Flip the finished edge of the binding over the raw edge of the quilt and slipstitch the binding to the back of the quilt. Trim the ends even with the edge of the quilt, as shown.

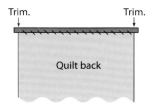

Stitch binding and trim.

3. For the 2 remaining sides of the quilt, measure the length of the quilt from top to bottom. Piece or trim 2 binding strips to this measurement plus 1˝. Sew the binding strips to the sides of the quilt. Fold the binding to the back of the quilt, trim the excess to ¼˝ on each end, and tuck in the overhang. Slipstitch the binding to the back of the quilt. Also slipstitch the tucked end.

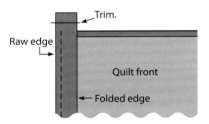

Attach side binding.

Double-Fold Binding with Mitered Corners

With raw edges even, pin the binding to the front edge of the quilt, a few inches away from a corner. Leave the first few inches of the binding unattached. Start sewing, using a ¼˝ seam allowance.

Stop ¼˝ away from the first corner (see Step 1), and backstitch one stitch. Lift the presser foot and needle. Rotate the quilt one-quarter turn. Fold the binding at a right angle so it extends straight above the quilt and the fold forms a 45° angle in the corner (see Step 2). Then bring the binding strip down even with the edge of the quilt (see Step 3). Begin sewing at the folded edge. Repeat in the same manner at all corners.

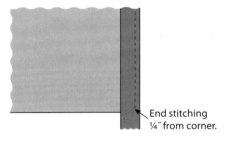

Step 1. Stitch to ¼˝ from corner.

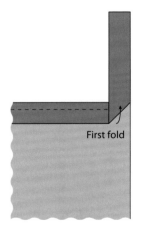

Step 2. First fold for miter

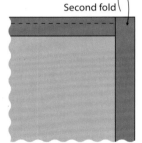

Step 3. Second fold alignment

Continue stitching until you are back near the beginning of the binding strip. See Finishing the Binding Ends for tips on finishing and hiding the raw edges of the ends of the binding.